FOURTH EDITION

1B

Series Director: **Diane Larsen-Freeman**

Grammar Dimensions

Form • Meaning • Use

Victoria Badalamenti

Carolyn Henner-Stanchina

THOMSON

HEINLE

Australia • Canada • Mexico • Singapore • Spain • United Kingdom • United States

THOMSON

™

HEINLE

Series Director: Diane Larsen-Freeman
Grammar Dimensions 1B: Form, Meaning, and Use
Victoria Badalamenti, Carolyn Henner-Stanchina

Publisher: *Sherrise Roehr*
Consulting Editor: *James W. Brown*
Director of Content Development: *Anita Raducanu*
Acquisitions Editor, Academic ESL: *Tom Jefferies*
Director of Product Marketing: *Amy Mabley*
Executive Marketing Manager: *Jim McDonough*
Senior Field Marketing Manager: *Donna Lee Kennedy*
Assistant Marketing Manager: *Caitlin Driscoll*
Assistant Editor: *Sarah Spader*

Editorial Assistants: *Katherine Reilly, Emily Dendinger*
Senior Production Editor: *Maryellen Eschmann-Killeen*
Senior Print Buyer: *Mary Beth Hennebury*
Development Editors: *Yeny Kim, Sarah Barnicle*
Production Project Manager: *Chrystie Hopkins*
Production Services: *Pre-Press Company, Inc.*
Interior Designer: *Lori Stuart*
Cover Designer: *Studio Montage*
Printer: *R.R. Donnelley*

Cover Image: © John Lawrence/Photographer's Choice/Getty

Printed in the United States of America.
1 2 3 4 5 6 7 8 9 10 — 11 10 09 08 07

For more information contact Thomson Heinle, 25 Thomson
Place, Boston, Massachusetts 02210 USA, or you can visit
our Internet site at http://elt.thomson.com

Credits appear on pages C-1–C-2, which constitutes a
continuation of the copyright page.

For permission to use material from this text or product, submit
a request online at http://www.thomsonrights.com

Any additional questions about permissions can be submitted
by email to thomsonrights@thomson.com

ISBN 10: 1-4240-0337-7
ISBN 13: 978-1-4240-0337-2

International Student Edition
ISBN 10: 1-4240-0839-5
ISBN 13: 978-1-4240-0839-1

CONTENTS

Unit 12   Adverbs of Manner 188

Unit 13   Direct and Indirect Objects, Direct and Indirect Object Pronouns 198

Unit 14   *Can, Know How To, Be Able To,* Connectors: *And/But/So/Or* 216

A Word from Diane Larsen-Freeman, Series Editor

Before *Grammar Dimensions* was published, teachers would ask me, "What is the role of grammar in a communicative approach?" These teachers recognized the importance of teaching grammar, but they associated grammar with form and communication with meaning, and thus could not see how the two easily fit together. *Grammar Dimensions* was created to help teachers and students appreciate the fact that grammar is not just about form. While grammar does indeed involve form, in order to communicate, language users also need to know the meaning of the forms and when to use them appropriately. In fact, it is sometimes not the form, but the *meaning* or *appropriate use* of a grammatical structure that represents the greatest long-term learning challenge for students. For instance, learning when it is appropriate to use the present perfect tense instead of the past tense, or being able to use two-word or phrasal verbs meaningfully, represent formidable challenges for English language learners.

The three dimensions of *form*, *meaning*, and *use* can be depicted in this pie chart with their interrelationship illustrated by the three arrows.

Helping students learn to use grammatical structures accurately, meaningfully, and appropriately is the fundamental goal of *Grammar Dimensions.* It is consistent with the goal of helping students to communicate meaningfully in English, and one that recognizes the undeniable interdependence of grammar and communication.

Enjoy the Fourth Edition of *Grammar Dimensions*!

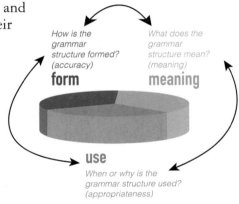

How is the grammar structure formed? (accuracy)
form

What does the grammar structure mean? (meaning)
meaning

use
When or why is the grammar structure used? (appropriateness)

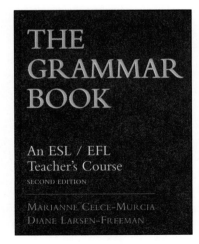

THE GRAMMAR BOOK

An ESL / EFL Teacher's Course
SECOND EDITION

MARIANNE CELCE-MURCIA
DIANE LARSEN-FREEMAN

To learn more about form, meaning, and use, read *The Grammar Book: An ESL/EFL Teacher's Course,* Second Edition, by Marianne Celce-Murcia and Diane Larsen-Freeman. ISBN: 0-8384-4725-2.

To learn about theory that has informed *Grammar Dimensions,* consult *Teaching Language: From Grammar to Grammaring,* also by Diane Larsen-Freeman. ISBN: 0-8384-6675-3.

Welcome to *Grammar Dimensions,* Fourth Edition!

The **clearest**, most **comprehensive** and **communicative** grammar series available! The fourth edition of *Grammar Dimensions* is more **user-friendly** and makes teaching grammar more **effective** than ever.

GRAMMAR DIMENSIONS IS COMPREHENSIVE AND CLEAR.

Grammar Dimensions systematically addresses the three dimensions of language—form, meaning, and use—through clear and comprehensive grammar explanations and extensive practice exercises. Each unit methodically focuses on each students' dimension and then integrates what they have learned in end-of-unit activities. In addition, grammatical structures are recycled throughout the series allowing students to practice and build upon their existing knowledge.

GRAMMAR DIMENSIONS IS COMMUNICATIVE.

Grammar Dimensions includes a large variety of lively communicative and personalized activities throughout each unit, eliciting self-expression and personalized practice. Interactive activities at the start of each unit serve as diagnostic tools directing student learning towards the most challenging dimensions of language structure. Integrated activities at the end of each unit include reading, writing, listening, and speaking activities allowing students to practice grammar and communication in tandem. New research activities encourage students to use authentic Internet resources and to reflect on their own learning.

GRAMMAR DIMENSIONS IS USER-FRIENDLY AND FLEXIBLE.

Grammar Dimensions has been designed to be flexible. Instructors can use the units in order or as set by their curriculum. Exercises can be used in order or as needed by the students. In addition, a tight integration between the Student Book, the Workbook, and the Lesson Planner makes teaching easier and makes the series more user-friendly.

GRAMMAR DIMENSIONS IS EFFECTIVE.

Students who learn the form, meaning, and use of each grammar structure will be able to communicate more accurately, meaningfully, and appropriately.

New to the Fourth Edition

- **NEW and revised grammar explanations** and examples help students and teachers easily understand and comprehend each language structure.

- **NEW and revised grammar charts and exercises** provide a wealth of opportunities for students to practice and master their new language.

- **NEW thematically and grammatically related Internet activities in** book 1 and *InfoTrac® College Edition activities* in every unit of books 2, 3, and 4 develop student research using current technologies.

- **NEW Reflection activities** encourage students to create personal language goals and to develop learning strategies.

- **NEW design, art, and photos** make each activity and exercise more engaging.

- **NEW Lesson Planners** assist both beginning and experienced teachers in giving their students the practice and skills they need to communicate accurately, meaningfully, and appropriately. All activities and exercises in the Lesson Planner are organized into step-by-step lessons so that no instructor feel overwhelmed.

SEQUENCING OF *GRAMMAR DIMENSIONS*

In *Grammar Dimensions* students progress from the sentence level to the discourse level, and learn to communicate appropriately at all levels.

Grammar Dimensions Book 1   *Grammar Dimensions* Book 2   *Grammar Dimensions* Book 3   *Grammar Dimensions* Book 4

Sentence level   Discourse level

	Book 1	**Book 2**	**Book 3**	**Book 4**
Level	High-beginning	Intermediate	High-Intermediate	Advanced
Grammar level	Sentence and sub-sentence level	Sentence and sub-sentence level	Discourse level	Discourse level
Primary language and communication focus	Semantic notions such as *time* and *place*	Social functions, such as *making requests* and *seeking* permission	Cohesion and coherence at the discourse level	Academic and technical discourse
Major skill focus	Listening and speaking	Listening and speaking	Reading and writing	Reading and writing

Guided Tour of *Grammar Dimensions 1*

Unit goals **provide a roadmap** for the grammar points students will work on.

"Opening Task" can be used as a **diagnostic warm-up** exercise to explore students' knowledge of each structure.

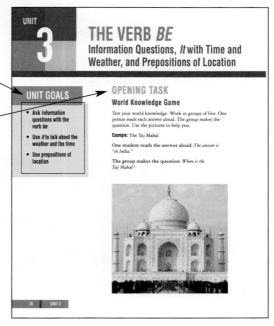

UNIT 3

THE VERB *BE*
Information Questions, *It* with Time and Weather, and Prepositions of Location

UNIT GOALS

- Ask information questions with the verb *be*
- Use *it* to talk about the weather and the time
- Use prepositions of location

OPENING TASK
World Knowledge Game

Test your world knowledge. Work in groups of five. One person reads each answer aloud. The group makes the question. Use the pictures to help you.

Example: The Taj Mahal

One student reads the answer aloud: *The answer is "in India."*

The group makes the question: *Where is the Taj Mahal?*

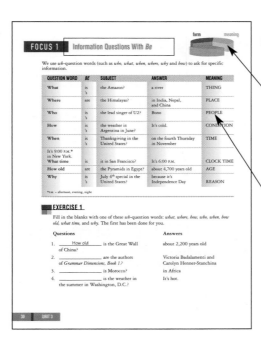

"Focus" sections present the **form, meaning,** and/or **use** of a particular structure helping students develop the skill of "**grammaring**"—the ability to use structures accurately, meaningfully, and appropriately.

Clear grammar charts present multiple examples, so teachers can have students work inductively to try to discover the rule on their own. More challenging grammar parts are accompanied by complete explanations.

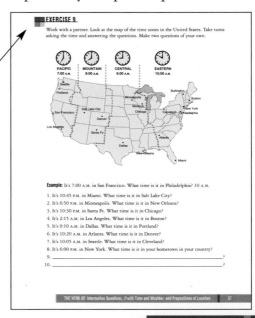

Purposeful exercises provide a wealth of opportunity for students to practice and personalize the grammar.

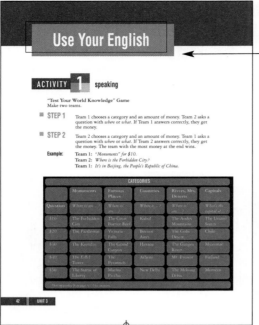

The "**Use Your English**" section (fondly known as the purple pages) offers communicative activities that **integrate grammar with reading, writing, listening, and speaking skills.** Communicative activities consolidate grammar instruction with enjoyable and meaningful tasks.

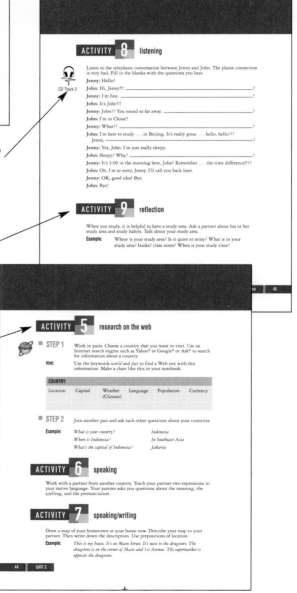

Engaging listening activities on audio cassette and audio CD further reinforce the target structure.

Reflection activities help students understand their learning style and create learning strategies.

Research activity using the Internet encourages students to read articles on carefully selected topics and use this information to reflect on a theme or on information studied in each unit.

Supplements

These additional components help teachers teach and student learn to use English grammar structures accurately.

The Lesson Planner

The lesson planner facilitates teaching by providing detailed lesson plans and examples, answer keys to the Student Book and Workbook, references to all of the components, and the tapescript for the audiocassette activities. The Lesson Planner minimizes teacher preparation time by providing:

- Summary of main grammar points for the teacher
- Information for the teacher on typical student errors
- Step-by-step guidelines for every focus box, exercise, and activity
- Suggested correlations between exercises and activities in the Use Your English pages
- Suggested timing for each exercise and each lesson
- Lead-in suggestions and examples for focus boxes
- Suggestions for expansion work follow most exercises
- Balance of cognitive and communicative activities
- Explanation for the teacher of the purpose of each activity, in order to differentiate cognitive from communicative emphasis
- Occasional methodology notes to anticipate possible procedural problems.

Assessment CD-ROM with *ExamView® Pro* Test Generator

The Assessment CD-ROM allows instructors to **create customized quizzes and tests** quickly and easily from a test bank of questions. Monitoring student understanding and progress has never been easier! The answer key appears with instructor copies of each quiz or test created.

Audio Program

Audio cassettes and CDs **provide listening activities for** each unit so students can practice listening to **grammar structures.**

Workbook

Workbooks **provide additional exercises** for each grammar point presented in the student text. Also offers editing practice and questions types found on many language exams.

Web site

Features additional grammar practice activities: elt.thomson.com/grammardimensions.

Empirical and Experiential Support for the *Grammar Dimensions* Approach

Opening Task Activities

The approach to teaching grammar used in the *Grammar Dimensions* series is well-grounded empirically and experientially. The Opening Task in each unit situates the learning challenge and allows students to participate in and learn from activity right from the beginning (Greeno 2006). In addition, students don't enter the classroom as empty vessels, waiting to be filled (Sawyer 2006). By observing how students perform on the Opening Task, teachers can analyze for themselves what students know and are able to do and what they don't know or are not able to do. Teachers can thus select from each unit what is necessary for students to build on from what they already bring with them.

Consciousness-Raising Exercises and Focus Boxes

Many of the exercises in *Grammar Dimensions* are of the consciousness-raising sort, where students are invited to make observations about some aspect of the target structure. This type of activity promotes students' noticing (Schmidt 1990), an important step in acquiring the grammar structure. The Focus Boxes further encourage this noticing, this time very explicitly. Explicit formulations of the sort found in the Focus Boxes can lead to implicit acquisition with practice (DeKeyser 1998). Moreover, certain learners (those with analytic learning styles) benefit greatly from explicit treatment of grammar structures (Larsen-Freeman and Long 1991).

Productive Practice and Communicative Activities

However, noticing by itself is insufficient. In order to be able to use the grammar structure, students need productive practice (Gatbonton and Segalowitz 1988; Larsen-Freeman 2003). Therefore, many of the exercises in *Grammar Dimensions* are of the output practice sort. Furthermore, each unit ends with communicative activities, where attention to the grammar is once again implicit, but where students can use the grammar structure in "psychologically authentic" or meaningful ways. Psychological authenticity is very important in order for students to be able to transfer what they know to new situations so that they can use it for their own purposes (Blaxton 1989) and so they are not left to contend with the "inert knowledge problem," (Whitehead 1929) where they know about the grammar, but can't use it.

The Three Dimensions of Grammar: Form, Meaning, and Use

Finally, applied linguistics research (Celce-Murcia and Larsen-Freeman 1999) supports the fundamental premise underlying *Grammar Dimensions:* that knowing a grammar structure means being able to use it accurately, meaningfully, and appropriately. Form focus or meaning focus by itself is insufficient (Larsen-Freeman 2001); all three dimensions—form, meaning, and use—need to be learned.

References

Blaxton, T. (1989). Investigating dissociations among memory measures: Support for a transfer-appropriate processing framework. *Journal of Experimental Psychology: Learning, Memory, and Cognition 15 (4): 657-668.*

Celce-Murcia, M. and D. Larsen-Freeman. (1999). *The grammar bbook: An ESL/EFL teacher's course.* Second Edition. Boston: Heinle & Heinle.

De Keyser, R. (1998). Beyond focus on form: Cognitive perspectives on learning and practicing second language grammar. n C. Doughty and J. Williams (eds.), *Focus on Classroom Second Language Acquisition.* Cambridge: Cambridge University Press, 42–63.

Gatbonton, E. and N. Segalowitz. (1988). Creative automatization: Principles for promoting fluency within a communicative framework. *TESOL Quarterly 22 (3):* 473–492.

Greeno, J. (2006). Learning in activity. In R. K. Sawyer (ed.), *The Cambridge handbook of learning sciences.* Cambridge: Cambridge University Press, 79–96.

Larsen-Freeman, D. (2001). Teaching grammar. In M. Celce-Murcia (ed.), *Teaching English as a Second or Foreign Language.* Third edition. Boston: Heinle & Heinle, 251–266.

Larsen-Freeman, D. (2003). *Teaching language: From grammar to grammaring.* Boston: Heinle & Heinle.

Larsen-Freeman, D. and M. Long. (1991). *An introduction to second language qcquisition research.* London: Longman.

Sawyer, R. K. (2006). Introduction: The new science of learning. In R. K. Sawyer (ed.), *The Cambridge handbook of learning sciences.* Cambridge: Cambridge University Press, 1–16.

Schmidt, R. (1990). The role of consciousness in second language learning. *Applied Linguistics 11 (2), 129–158.*

Whitehead, A. N. 1929. *The aims of education.* New York: MacMillan.

Acknowledgments from the Series Director

This fourth edition would not have come about if it had not been for the enthusiastic response of teachers and students using all the previous editions. I am very grateful for the reception *Grammar Dimensions* has been given.

I am also grateful for all the authors' efforts. To be a teacher, and at the same time a writer, is a difficult balance to achieve . . . so is being an innovative creator of materials, and yet, a team player. They have met these challenges exceedingly well in my opinion. Then, too, the Thomson Heinle team has been impressive. I am grateful for the leadership exercised by Jim Brown, Sherrise Roehr, and Tom Jefferies. I also appreciate all the support from Anita Raducanu, Amy Mabley, Sarah Barnicle, Laura Needham, Chrystie Hopkins, Mary Beth Hennebury, and Abigail Greshik of Pre-Press Company. Deserving special mention are Amy Lawler and Yeny Kim, who never lost the vision while they attended to the detail with good humor and professionalism.

I have also benefited from the counsel of Marianne Celce-Murcia, consultant for the first edition of this project, and my friend. Finally, I wish to thank my family members, Elliott, Brent, and Gavin, for not once asking the (negative yes-no) question that must have occurred to them countless times: "Haven't you finished yet?" As we all have discovered, this project has a life of its own and is never really finished! And, for this, I am exceedingly grateful. Happy Grammaring all!

A Special Thanks

The series director, authors, and publisher would like to thank the following reviewers whose experienced observations and thoughtful suggestions have assisted us in creating and revising *Grammar Dimensions*.

Michelle Alvarez
University of Miami
Coral Gables, Florida

Edina Pingleton Bagley
Nassau Community College
Garden City, New York

Jane Berger
Solano Community College,
California

Mary Bottega
San Jose State University

Mary Brooks
Eastern Washington
University

Christina Broucqsault
California State Polytechnic
University

José Carmona
Hudson Community College

Susan Carnell
University of Texas at Arlington

Susana Christie
San Diego State University

Diana Christopher
Georgetown University

Gwendolyn Cooper
Rutgers University

Julia Correia
Henderson State University
Arkadelphia, Arkansas

Sue Cozzarelli
EF International,
San Diego

Catherine Crystal
Laney College, California

Kevin Ccross
University of San Francisco

Julie Damron
Interlink at Valparaiso
University, Indiana

Glen Deckert
Eastern Michigan
University

Eric Dwyer
University of Texas
at Austin

Nikki Ellman
Laney College
Oakland, California

Ann Eubank
Jefferson Community College

Alice Fine
UCLA Extension

Alicia Going
The English Language Study
Center, Oregon

Molly Gould
University of Delaware

Maren M. Hargis
San Diego Mesa College

Penny Harrold
Universidad de Monterrey
Monterrey, Mexico

Robin Hendrickson
Riverside City College
Riverside, California

Mary Herbert
University of California,
Davis Extension

Jane Hilbert
*ELS Language Center,
Florida International
University*

Eli Hinkel
Xavier University

Kathy Hitchcox
*International English
Institute, Fresno*

Abeer Hubi
Altarbia Alislamia Schools
Riyadh, Saudi Arabia

Joyce Hutchings
Georgetown University

Heather Jeddy
*Northern Virginia
Community College*

Judi Keen
*University of California,
Davis,* and *Sacramento
City College*

Karli Kelber
*American Language Institute,
New York University*

Anne Kornfield
*LaGuardia Community
College*

Kay Longmire
*Interlink at Valparaiso
University, Indiana*

Robin Longshaw
*Rhode Island School
of Design*

Robert Ludwiczak
Texas A&M University
College Station, Texas

Bernadette McGlynn
*ELS Language Center, St.
Joseph's University*

Billy McGowan
Aspect International, Boston

Margaret Mehran
Queens College

Richard Moore
University of Washington

Karen Moreno
*Teikyo Post University,
Connecticut*

Gino Muzzetti
*Santa Rosa Junior College,
California*

Mary Nance-Tager
*LaGuardia Community
College, City University
of New York*

So Nguyen
Orange Coast College
Costa Mesa, California

Karen O'Neill
San Jose State University

Mary O'Neal
*Northern Virginia
Community College*

Nancy Pagliara
*Northern Virginia
Community College*

Keith Pharis
Southern Illinois University

Amy Parker
*ELS Language Center,
San Francisco*

Margene Petersen
*ELS Language Center,
Philadelphia*

Nancy Pfingstag
*University of North Carolina,
Charlotte*

Sally Prieto
*Grand Rapids Community
College*

India Plough
Michigan State University

Mostafa Rahbar
*University of Tennessee at
Knoxville*

Dudley Reynolds
Indiana University

Dzidra Rodins
DePaul University
Chicago, Illinois

Ann Salzman
*University of Illinois at
Urbana-Champaign*

Jennifer Schmidt
*San Francisco State
University*

Cynthia Schuemann
*Miami-Dade Community
College*

Jennifer Schultz
*Golden Gate University,
California*

Mary Beth Selbo
*Wright College, City Colleges
of Chicago*

Mary Selseleh
American River College
Sacramento, California

Stephen Sheeran
*Bishop's University,
Lenoxville, Quebec*

Kathy Sherak
*San Francisco State
University*

Sandra E. Sklarew
Merritt Community College
Oakland, California

Keith Smith
*ELS Language Center, San
Francisco*

Helen Solorzano
Northeastern University

Jorge Vazquez Solorzano
*Bachillerato de la Reina de
Mexico*
S. C., Mexico, D. F.,
Mexico

Christina Valdez
Pasadena City College
Pasadena, California

Danielle Valentini
Oakland Community College
Farmington Hills, Michigan

Amelia Yongue
Howard Community College
Columbia, Maryland

CAN, KNOW HOW TO, BE ABLE TO, CONNECTORS: AND/BUT/SO/OR

UNIT GOALS

- Use *can* to express ability

- Ask questions with *can*

- Ask for help with English using *can*

- Understand the difference between *can/know how to/be able to* for expressing learned or natural ability

- Use sentence connectors: *and, but, so,* and *or* correctly

OPENING TASK

In his book *Frames of Mind*, about multiple intelligences, Howard Gardner defines different types of intelligences.

■ STEP 1

Read the statements related to six of Gardner's types of intelligence. Check the things that you can do. Then ask your partner questions about your partner's ability.

	ME ...	MY PARTNER ...
1. Visual Intelligence ("Picture" Smart)		
a. do a puzzle		
b. interpret a graph		
c. read a map		
2. Verbal Intelligence ("Word" Smart)		
a. tell a story		
b. speak three languages		
c. write		
3. Physical Intelligence ("Body" Smart)		
a. dance		
b. play sports		
c. act		

	ME ...	MY PARTNER ...
4. Musical Intelligence ("Music" Smart)		
a. sing		
b. play a musical instrument		
c. write music		
5. Logical Intelligence ("Logic" Smart)		
a. work with numbers and shapes		
b. think scientifically		
c. solve problems with logic		
6. Interpersonal Intelligence ("People" Smart)		
a. work well in a group		
b. understand others		
c. communicate with all kinds of people		

■ STEP 2

Ask your partner questions about his/her abilities. What type of intelligence do you think your partner has? Tell the class why.

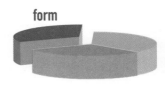

form

FOCUS 1   *Can*

Can is a special kind of verb called a modal verb. Modal verbs come before the base form of the verb. Modals do not take *-s* in the third person singular (with subjects he-she-it). *Can* expresses ability.

AFFIRMATIVE	NEGATIVE	NEGATIVE CONTRACTION
I You He She **can** speak English. We You They	I You He She **cannot** speak Chinese. We You They	I You He She **can't** speak French. We You They
(a) She can DANCE. (b) He can SING.	In the affirmative, we pronounce *can* as /ken/ and stress the base form of the verb.	
(c) He CAN'T DANCE. (d) She CAN'T SING.	In the negative, we stress both *can't* and the base form of the verb.	

EXERCISE 1

Go back to the Opening Task on pages 216–217. With a partner, take turns saying what you can or can't do.

Examples: *I can read a map.*
I can't play a musical instrument.

EXERCISE 2

"Musical Savants" are special people. They have some social, learning, and physical disabilities, but they also have one extraordinary ability. For example, Eric is a blind musical savant.

Complete the sentences with an affirmative or a negative form of *can* and a verb in the box.

create	remember	play	write	communicate	read

1. He _____ .

2. He _____ .

3. He _____ the piano.

4. He _____ any new music he hears, and he
can play it.

5. He _____ new music.

6. He _____ through music.

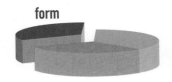

form

FOCUS 2   Questions with *Can*

YES/NO QUESTIONS	INFORMATION QUESTIONS
(a) **Can** you use a computer? Yes, I can. / No, I can't.	(c) What **can** you do on the computer? I can do research on the Internet.
(b) **Can** he cook? Yes, he can. / No, he can't.	(d) Who **can** cook in your family? My mother can. My father can't boil water!

EXERCISE 3

STEP 1   Write *yes/no* questions with *can*. Then, under *Your Response,* check *Yes* or *No* to give your opinion about each question. Leave the columns under *Total* blank for now.

	YOUR RESPONSE		TOTAL	
	YES	NO	YES	NO
1. a woman/work as a firefighter <u>Can a woman work as a firefighter?</u>				
2. women/fight bravely in wars _____?				
3. a man/be a good nurse _____?				
4. men/raise children _____?				
5. women/be good police officers _____?				
6. a woman/be a construction worker _____?				
7. a man/keep house neatly _____?				
8. a woman/be a good leader of a country _____?				
9. men/communicate well with women _____?				

STEP 2   Go back to Step 1. Read the questions aloud. Do a survey in your class. Count how many students say "yes" and how many say "no." Write the *total* number of *Yes* and *No* answers in the *Total* column. Do you agree or disagree with your classmates? Give reasons for your answers.

Example: *Women can be good police officers. They can be tough. They can be brave.*
They can help people in trouble.

EXERCISE 4

Work in a group of four to six people. Find out who in your group can do the following things. Take turns asking the questions. Keep the conversation going by asking follow-up questions. Report the results to your class.

Example: Who/type?
Student 1: Who can type?
Student 2: I can type.
Student 1: How fast can you type?
Student 2: I can type 90 words per minute.

1. Who/cook? _____

_____

2. Who/speak more than one language? _____

_____

3. Who/play a musical instrument? _____

_____

4. Who/solve math problems? _____

_____

5. Who/teach? _____

_____

6. Who/draw? _____

_____

7. Who/run a marathon? _____

_____

8. Who/play card games? _____

_____

use

EXAMPLES	EXPLANATIONS
(a) **Can I say,** "She can to swim" **in English?**	When you are not sure your English is correct, use the expression: *Can I say . . . in English?*
(b) **A:** How can I say, ". . ." in English?  B: That's called "sweeping."	When you don't know how to say something in English, ask the question: *How can I say, ". . ." in English?*

EXERCISE 5

Look at the pictures. First, mime each action. Then ask your classmates questions to find out how to say each word. Do three of your own.

Example: *How can I say* (mime the action) *in English?*

1.

2.

3.

4.

5.

6.

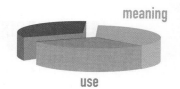

FOCUS 4 — Expressing Ability: *Can, Know How to,* and *Be Able to*

EXAMPLES	EXPLANATIONS
(a) She **can** cook. (b) She **knows how to** cook. (c) She **is able to** cook.	To express learned ability, use *can, know how to,* or *be able to.*
(d) A blind person **can't** see. (e) A blind person **isn't able to** see. (f) NOT: A blind person **doesn't know how to** see.	To express natural ability, use *can* or *be able to* only. *Be able to* is more formal than *can.* Use *be able to* in all tenses; not *can.*

EXERCISE 6

Make affirmative or negative statements with the words below. To express <u>learned</u> ability, make one statement with *can / can't* and one statement with *know(s) how to / don't/doesn't know how to.* To express <u>natural</u> ability, make only one statement with *can/can't.*

Examples: a. A chef/cook
   A chef can cook.
   A chef knows how to cook.

   b. Humans/learn a new language
   Humans can learn a new language.

1. A blind person/see

2. A dog/live for twenty-five years

3. Infants/walk

4. A deaf person/hear

5. Fish/breathe on land

6. A man/have a baby

7. Doctors/cure all diseases

8. Men/take care of babies

9. Roses/grow without water

10. Painters/work with color and light

EXERCISE 7

Fill in the blanks in the sentences. For <u>learned</u> ability, use the affirmative or negative form of *be able to*. For <u>natural</u> ability, use the affirmative or negative form of *can*.

Evelyn Glennie is a Scottish percussion musician. She (1) _____ play over 1,800 percussion instruments. Surprisingly, Evelyn Glennie is also profoundly deaf. Being "profoundly deaf" means she (2) _____ hear only a little. She (3) _____ hear the sounds of people speaking, but she (4) _____ understand the words. Evelyn (5) _____ read lips to understand people's words, but how can she be a musician? Evelyn (6) _____ hear music with her ears. But she believes that hearing is a form of touching. When our ears don't work, we (7) _____ feel the sound vibrations. In this way, a deaf person (8) _____ touch sounds. Evelyn (9) _____ also see sounds. When she sees something move or vibrate, she (10) _____ create that sound in her mind. Evelyn Glennie (11) _____ hear. But she (12) _____ perform at international concerts. She (13) _____ teach. She (14) _____ communicate with people through the language of music. Evelyn Glennie is an amazing musician.

EXERCISE 8

Test your knowledge. Make *yes/no* questions with *be able to*. Then discuss your answers.

Example: people/live without food and water for one month
Are people able to live without food and water for one month?
No, they aren't. People are able to live without food for one month. But they aren't able to live without water for one month.

1. a computer/think

   _____

2. robots/raise children

   _____

3. an airplane/fly from New York to Paris in four hours

   _____

4. cats/see in the dark

   _____

5. a river/flow uphill

   _____

6. we/communicate with people from other planets

   _____

7. a person/learn a language in one week

   _____

8. doctors/cure AIDS

   _____

9. a 2-year old child/read

   _____

10. the United Nations/stop wars

    _____

11. humans/travel to outer space

    _____

12. you/think of any more questions

    _____

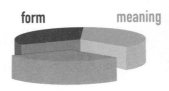

FOCUS 5   Sentence Connectors: *And/But/So/Or*

And, but, so, and or are sentence connectors. We use them to connect two complete sentences.

EXAMPLES	EXPLANATIONS
(a) I can roller-skate, **and** I can ski.	**And** adds information.
(b) I can dance, **but** I can't sing. He can swim, **but** his brother can't.	**But** shows contrast.
(c) I can't cook, **so** I often go out to eat.	**So** gives a result.
(d) You can go, **or** you can stay.	**Or** gives a choice.
(e) I can speak English, but I can't speak Chinese. (f) I can speak Spanish, and my sister can speak Japanese.	When you connect two complete sentences, use a comma (,) before the connector.
(g) I can say it in English, or I can say it in French. (h) I can say it in English or French.	When the subject is the same for the two verbs, it is not necessary to repeat the subject or *can*.
(i) **Nick** can watch a movie, or **he** can play soccer.	When the subject is the same for the two verbs, you can use a pronoun in the second clause.
(j) My sister can play the piano, but I **can't**. (k) I'm able to eat spicy food, but my wife **isn't**. (l) Jim knows how to fix computer problems, but Ted **doesn't**.	When the subjects are different but the verb is the same, it is not necessary to repeat the base form of the verb (e.g., *play the piano, eat spicy food, fix computer problems*).

EXERCISE 9

You want to spend a Saturday with a classmate. Choose a partner. Ask each other questions to decide what kind of day you want to have. Then add three questions of your own.

Example: **You:** *Do you want to meet early for breakfast or wait until later to meet?*
Your partner: *Let's meet early for breakfast.*

1. meet early for breakfast/wait until later to meet
2. skip lunch/have a picnic lunch
3. go to a museum/spend some time outdoors (in a park or at the beach)
4. surf the Internet/play soccer
5. cook dinner together/eat out
6. rent a DVD/go to a movie
7. _____
8. _____
9. _____

EXERCISE 10

How technologically smart are you? Write sentences using *can* or *know how to* with *and* or *but*.

1. take a photo/edit a digital photo
2. write a check/ do banking online
3. listen to a CD/burn a CD
4. use a computer/write a computer program
5. surf the Web/evaluate good Web sources for a research project
6. use an MP3 player/download music
7. play the piano/play an electronic keyboard
8. send an e-mail/send an attachment to an e-mail
9. chat online/send a text message

Fill in the blanks with *and, but, so,* or *or.*

Daniel Tammet is a mathematical savant. He lives in England. He can multiply big numbers in his head. He loves numbers (a) _____ loves to count, (b) _____ the problem is, he can't stop. He tries to count the pebbles at the beach, (c) _____ there are too many pebbles to count, (d) _____ Daniel gets tired. As a result he doesn't like the beach. At the supermarket, Daniel counts every fruit (e) _____ every vegetable, (f) _____ he doesn't like the supermarket. Daniel is a mathematical genius, (g) _____ he can't drive a car (h) _____ understand people's feelings.

   Daniel can never change his daily schedule. He needs to brush his teeth (i) _____ drink his tea at the same time every day, (j) _____ it is difficult for Daniel to keep a regular job.

   Like Eric in Exercise 2, Daniel has extraordinary abilities, (k) _____ he also has extraordinary disabilities.

Use Your English

ACTIVITY **1** speaking

Read the job advertisement in the newspaper for a baby sitter. Interview your partner for the job. Ask questions with *can, know how to,* and *be able to.*

Examples: *Do you know how to cook?*

Can you work full-time?

142 Employment

WANTED: Baby sitter ★
Responsible person. Full-tme work five days a week 8:00-5:00, some evenings and weekends. Must speak English and be able to drive. Laundry, light housekeeping, and cooking required. Experience with children necessary. References requested.

ACTIVITY **2** writing

What can you do that your parents or other people you know cannot do? Write six sentences.

Examples: *My mother can't ride a bicycle, but I can.*

My sister knows how to sew, but I don't.

ACTIVITY **3** writing/speaking

Do you think it's better to be a man or a woman? Write as many reasons as you can for your opinion, and then discuss them.

Example: *It's better to be a woman. A woman can have children.*

ACTIVITY 4 speaking

Make a list of ten jobs. Say what you can or are able to do. The class decides what job is good for you. Use *and* and *but*.

Example: **You say:** *I can help sick people and get along with them. I am able to follow directions.*

Your group: *Then you can be a nurse!*

ACTIVITY 5 speaking

■ **STEP 1** Ask a classmate if he or she can do one of the activities in the box below.

Example: *Can you touch your toes without bending your knees?*

■ **STEP 2** If the person says *yes*, write his/her name in the box. Then go to another student and ask another question.

If the person says *no*, ask the other questions until he or she says *yes*. Then write his or her name in the box.

■ **STEP 3** Each student who answered *yes* must perform the action!

touch your toes without bending your knees	dance salsa	whistle
————	————	————
sing a song in English	say "Hello" in four languages	tell a joke in English
————	————	————
draw a horse	pronounce this word: "psychology"	juggle
————	————	————

ACTIVITY 6 listening/speaking

CD Track 13

■ **STEP 1** Listen to Ken's interview for a job. Then read the statements. Check *Yes* or *No*.

	YES	NO
1. Ken can speak Spanish.		
2. Ken can understand Latin American people.		
3. Ken is able to listen to others patiently.		
4. Ken is able to understand people's needs.		
5. He can solve problems.		
6. He can cooperate with others.		
7. He can use a computer.		

■ **STEP 2** According to this conversation, what kind of intelligence does Ken have?

a. Musical   b. Interpersonal   c. Physical

ACTIVITY 7 reflection

■ **STEP 1** What can you do in English? Check *Yes* or *No*. Add two additional abilities.

	YES	NO
1. I am able to introduce someone.		
2. I know how to ask about prices.		
3. I can describe people and places.		
4. I can make a polite request.		
5. I'm able to give directions.		
6. I can give advice.		
7. I know how to ask for information about English.		
8. _____		
9. _____		

■ **STEP 2** Now, exchange books with a partner. Tell what your partner can or can't do in English.

Example: *My partner is able to introduce someone.*

PRESENT PROGRESSIVE TENSE

UNIT GOALS

- Make affirmative and negative statements in the present progressive tense

- Know how to spell verbs ending in *-ing*

- Choose between the simple present and the present progressive

- Know which verbs are not usually used in the progressive

- Ask *yes/no* questions in the present progressive

OPENING TASK

A Bad Day at the Harrisons'

Robin and Regis have three children. Their babysitter cannot come today, so Regis is staying at home and taking care of the children and the house.

Why is Regis having a bad day?

Talk about what is happening in the picture. Use the verbs in the box.

VERBS
bark
play cowboy on his father's back
burn
go crazy
watch TV
do homework
cry
ring
fight over a toy
walk into the apartment

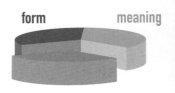

FOCUS 1 — Present Progressive: Affirmative Statements

EXAMPLES	EXPLANATIONS
(a) The food **is burning.** (b) The baby **is crying.** (c) The dog and the baby **are fighting.**	Use the present progressive to talk about an action that is happening right now; an action in progress.
(d) **The baby is crying and fighting** with the dog.	We usually do not repeat the subject and the verb *be* when the subject is doing two or more things.

SUBJECT	BE	BASE FORM OF THE VERB + -*ING*
I	am	
He She It	is	working.
We You They	are	

Affirmative Contractions

SUBJECT + *BE* CONTRACTION	BASE FORM OF THE VERB + -*ING*
I'm	
He's She's It's	working.
We're You're They're	

EXERCISE 1

Underline all the present progressive verbs in the text.

Example: *Regis <u>isn't having</u> a good day.*

Today is not a normal day at the Harrisons'. Usually, Robin's babysitter comes at 3:00 P.M., and Robin leaves for class. Robin teaches from 4:00 P.M. until 8:00 P.M., but today, Robin is attending an all-day meeting at the college. Her babysitter is sick today, so Regis is spending the day at home. He's taking care of the children and the house. He's trying very hard, but everything is going wrong. Regis isn't having a good day. Actually, poor Regis is going crazy. He's thinking about Robin. He's learning something today. It's not easy to stay home with the children. He's beginning to understand this.

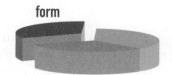

form

FOCUS 2	Spelling of Verbs Ending in *-ing*

VERB END	RULE	EXAMPLES	
1. consonant + *e*	Drop the *-e*, add *-ing*.	write	writing
2. consonant + vowel + consonant (one syllable verbs)	Double the consonant, add *-ing*.	sit	sitting
Exception: verbs that end in *-w, -x,* and *-y*.	Do not double *w, x,* and *y*.	show fix play	showing fixing playing
3. consonant + vowel + consonant. The verb has more than one syllable, and the stress is on the last syllable.	Double the consonant, add *-ing*.	beGIN forGET	beginning forgetting
If the stress is not on the last syllable	Do not double the consonant.	LISten HAPpen	listening happening
4. *-ie*	Change *-ie* to *y*, add *-ing*.	lie die	lying dying
5. All other verbs	Add *-ing* to the base form of verb.	talk study do agree	talking studying doing agreeing

EXERCISE 2

Fill in the blanks with the present progressive.

Today's a normal day at the Harrisons'. It is 4:00. Robin (1) _____
(prepare) dinner in the kitchen. She (2) _____ (slice) onions and
(3) _____ (wipe) the tears from her eyes. The house is quiet, so she
(4) _____ (listen) to some music. She (5) _____ (think) about
her class tonight. She (6) _____ (wait) for her babysitter to arrive. The baby
(7) _____ (sleep). The dog (8) _____ (lie) on the floor and
(9) _____ (chew) on a bone. Jimmy (10) _____ (play)
with his toys. Suzy (11) _____ (clean) her room. Nothing unusual
(12) _____ (happen). Everything is under control.

EXERCISE 3

Trends in the Changing Family: Young Adults
Complete all the statements in columns A and B. Then find the statement in column B
that matches and explains each statement in column A. Read the two statements
together.

A	B
1. More and more, young people (move) _____ back home after college.	a. They (build) _____ their careers first, before getting married.
2. Young men and women (delay) _____ marriage.	b. The cost of raising a child (increase) _____.
3. Many young couples (live) _____ together, but they (not/get) _____ married.	c. Working mothers (feel) _____ too much stress.
4. Many families (get) _____ smaller.	d. Couples (worry) _____ about the high divorce rate.
5. Some women (quit) _____ their jobs to stay home with their children.	e. Young people (save) _____ money by living at home with their parents.

EXERCISE 4

Who's talking? Fill in the blanks with the present progressive of the verb. Then match each statement to a picture.

Example: *"You're* _____driving_____ *(drive)*
me crazy. Turn off the TV!"

1. "That crazy dog _____ (bite) me!"

a.

2. "What _____ (happen) here!
I _____ (walk) into a zoo!"

b.

3. "Quiet! You _____ (make) a lot of noise.
I can't hear the TV."

c.

4. "Stop that, Jimmy. You _____ (hurt) me."

d.

5. "Oh no! The food _____ (burn)!"

e.

6. "I _____ (die) to take off my shoes. My
feet _____ (kill) me."

f.

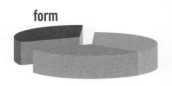

FOCUS 3 | Present Progressive: Negative Statements

SUBJECT + BE + NOT			NEGATIVE CONTRACTION			BE CONTRACTION + NOT		
I	am		*			I'm		
He			He			He's		
She	is		She	isn't		She's		
It's		not working.	It		working.	It's		not working.
We			We			We're		
You	are		You	aren't		You're		
They			They			They're		

*There is no standard English contraction with *I am not*.

EXERCISE 5

Make negative statements using contractions.

Example: Robin/take care of the children today.
Robin isn't taking care of the children today.

1. Robin/wear comfortable shoes today
2. Robin's babysitter/watch the children today
3. The baby and the dog/get along
4. Regis/pay attention to the dinner on the stove
5. The children/listen to Regis
6. Suzy/do her homework
7. Suzy/help Regis
8. Regis/laugh
9. Regis/relax
10. Regis/enjoy his children today

EXERCISE 6

Trends in the Changing Family: Older Adults

The term "baby boomer" refers to a person born in the United States between 1946 and 1964. After World War II, there was a "baby boom," or population explosion.

Read each statement. Make affirmative or negative statements in the present progressive.

1. Baby boomers (begin) _____ to turn 60.
2. They (try) _____ to stay young forever.
3. Some baby boomers (prepare) _____ to retire and relax.
4. They (plan) _____ to travel the world.
5. Others (not/seek) _____ to retire.
6. They (not/quit) _____ their jobs.
7. Some (think) _____ about changing careers.
8. They (go) _____ back to school to learn new skills.
9. They (hope) _____ to do interesting, meaningful work.
10. Some men (become) _____ fathers again at 60.
11. Other baby boomers (become) _____ grandparents.
12. Baby boomers (expect) _____ to live to 100!

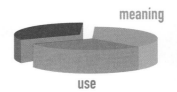

FOCUS 4 — Choosing Simple Present or Present Progressive

The simple present and the present progressive have different uses.

USE THE SIMPLE PRESENT FOR:	USE THE PRESENT PROGRESSIVE FOR:
• **habits and repeated actions** (a) Suzy usually does her homework in the evening.	• **actions in progress now** (c) Suzy's watching TV right now.
• **things that are true in general** (b) Women usually take care of children.	• **actions that are temporary, not habitual** (d) Regis is taking care of the children today. • **situations that are changing** (e) These days, men are spending more time with their children.

Time Expressions		Time Expressions	
always	*rarely*	*right now*	*now*
often	*never*	*today*	*at the moment*
usually	*every day/week/year*	*this week*	*this evening*
sometimes	*once a week*	*this year*	*this month*
seldom	*on the weekends*	*these days*	*nowadays*
all the time	*three times a year*		

EXERCISE 7

Read each statement. If the statement is in the simple present, make a second statement in the present progressive. If the statement is in the present progressive, make a second statement in the simple present. Discuss the differences in meaning.

SIMPLE PRESENT	PRESENT PROGRESSIVE
1a. Suzy usually does her homework in the evening.	1b. <u>Tonight she isn't doing her homework. She's watching cartoons.</u>
2a. _____	2b. Tonight, Robin isn't cooking dinner.
3a. Robin usually takes care of the children.	3b. _____
4a. _____	4b. Today, Regis is spending the day at home.
5a. The babysitter usually takes care of the children when Robin goes to work.	5b. _____

6a. _____ _____	6b. Right now, the baby and the dog are fighting.
7a. The babysitter doesn't usually go crazy.	7b. _____ _____
8a. Robin usually arrives home at 6:00 P.M.	8b. _____ _____

EXERCISE 8

Complete each statement with a verb in either the simple present or the present progressive. Be ready to explain your choice of verb.

In the traditional American family, men usually (1) _____ (work) and women (2) _____ (stay) home and (3) _____ (take) care of the children. Women (4) _____ (depend) on men financially.

Today, families (5) _____ (change). The roles of men and women (6) _____ (change), too. Nowadays, about 50 percent of American women (7) _____ (work) outside the home. Some women (8) _____ (get) high-paying jobs. Women (9) _____ (become) more financially independent. These days, some women (10) _____ (have) and (11) _____ (raise) children without men.

On the other hand, some married women with children and jobs (12) _____ (feel) stressed. These women (13) _____ (quit) their good jobs. They (14) _____ (stay) home with their children. Married men (15) _____ (share) the housework. They (16) _____ (help) their wives. They (17) _____ (spend) more time with their children.

Men and women (18) _____ (struggle) to balance work and family.

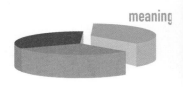

FOCUS 5 | Verbs Not Usually Used in the Progressive

There are some verbs we usually do not use in the present progressive. These verbs are *not* action verbs. They are called nonprogressive (or stative) verbs.

EXAMPLES	NONPROGRESSIVE (STATIVE) VERBS
(a) Robin **loves** her job. (b) NOT: Robin is loving her job. (c) The children **need** help. (d) NOT: The children are needing help.	**Feelings and Emotions** *(like, love, hate, prefer, want, need)*
(e) Regis **understands** his wife.	**Mental States** *(think, believe, understand, seem, forget, remember, know, mean)*
(f) Regis **hears** the telephone ringing.	**Senses** *(hear, see, smell, taste, feel, sound)*
(g) Robin and Regis **own** a house.	**Possession** *(belong, own, have)*

You can use the present progressive with some of these verbs, but they have a different meaning.

SIMPLE PRESENT	PRESENT PROGRESSIVE
(h) I **think** you're a good student. (*Think* means "believe.")	(i) I **am thinking** about you now. (Here *thinking* shows a mental action.)
(j) I **have** two cars. (*Have* means "possess.")	(k) I'm **having** a good time. (*Have* describes the experience.)
(l) This soup **tastes** delicious. (*Taste* means "has a delicious flavor.")	(m) I'm **tasting** the soup. (*Taste* here means the action of putting soup in one's mouth.)

EXERCISE 9

Fill in the blanks with the present progressive or simple present form of the verb. Read the dialogues aloud. Use contractions.

Example: **Regis:** *I'm going* (go) crazy in this house.
Robin: *I think* (think) you need a vacation!

1. **Regis:** Suzy, I need your help here.

    Suzy: But, Dad, you (a) _____ (need) my help every five minutes!
    I (b) _____ (watch) TV right now!

2. It is 3:00 P.M. The telephone rings.
    Regis: Hello.
    Laura: Hello, Regis. What are you doing home in the middle of the day?
    Regis: Oh, hi, Laura. I know I (a) _____ (be) never home during the
    day, but today I (b) _____ (try) to be a househusband!
    Laura: Oh really? Where's Robin?
    Regis: Robin (c) _____ (attend) a meeting at the college, so
    I (d) _____ (take) care of the kids.

3. Jimmy interrupts Regis's telephone conversation:
    Regis: Hold on a minute, Laura . . . Jimmy (a) _____ (pull) on my
    leg! Jimmy, I (b) _____ (talk) to Mommy's friend Laura
    right now. You (c) _____ (know) Laura. She
    (d) _____ (come) to see Mommy every week. Now, just wait
    a minute, please . . .
    Laura: Is everything O.K., Regis?
    Regis: Oh, yes. We (e) _____ (do) just fine. Bye!

4. It is 5:30 P.M. The telephone rings.
    Regis: Hello.
    Robin: Hi, honey! The meeting (a) _____ (be) over.
    I (b) _____ (be) on my way home. What
    (c) _____ (happen)? I hope the children
    (d) _____ (behave).
    Regis: They (e) _____ (behave) like wild animals, Robin.
    I (f) _____ (yell) at them all the time, but they don't listen to
    me. I (g) _____ (not/have) a very good day today.
    Robin: You (h) _____ (sound) terrible! Can I bring you anything?
    Regis: Yes, a bottle of aspirin!

EXERCISE 10

Work with a partner. Choose any picture (do not go in order). Describe the picture by making one statement with *seem, look,* or *feel* and an adjective from the box. Make another statement with the present progressive to say what the person is doing. Your partner must guess the number of the picture you are talking about. Take turns.

Example: **You say:** *The woman looks nervous. She's biting her nails.*
Your partner says: *Picture Number 5.*

sad	sick	scared	tired
angry	happy	cold	hot
bored	surprised	nervous	confused

1.

4.

7.

10.

2.

5.

8.

11.

3.

6.

9.

12.

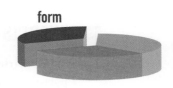

FOCUS 6 — Present Progressive: *Yes/No* Questions and Short Answers

YES/NO QUESTIONS			SHORT ANSWERS					
Am	I		Yes,	you	are.	No,	you	aren't.
Are	you		Yes,	I	am.	No,	I'm	not.
Is	he she it	working?	Yes,	he she it	is.	No,	he she it	isn't.
Are	we you they		Yes,	we you they	are.	No,	we you they	aren't.

EXERCISE 11

Refer to the picture in the Opening Task on page 233. With a partner, take turns asking and answering questions about the Harrisons. Give short answers. Use the verbs from the box below.

Example: Suzy / her father
You: *Is Suzy helping her father?*
Your partner: *No, she isn't.*

watch	ring	play	bite	come
enjoy	burn	help	fight	smile

1. children / their father
2. the baby and the dog
3. Suzy / TV
4. their dinner
5. the phone

6. Jimmy / cowboy
7. the dog / Regis
8. Robin / home
9. Robin
10. Regis / his children

Work with a partner. Ask your partner *yes/no* questions about changing trends in your partner's country. Add two questions of your own.

Example: young people / delay marriage *Are young adults delaying marriage in your country?*

1. couples / live together before marriage
2. women / stay home with their children
3. fathers / spend time with their children
4. men / share housework
5. women / become financially independent
6. women / raise children without men
7. more couples / get divorced
8. couples / pay babysitters to take care of their children
9. men and women / try to balance work and family
10. grandparents / live with their grown children and grandchildren
11. _____
12. _____

form

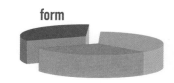

FOCUS 7	Present Progressive: *Wh*-Questions

WH-WORD	BE	SUBJECT	VERB + -*ING*	ANSWERS
What	am	I	doing?	(You're) getting ready for the beach.
When				(I'm going) at 2:00.
Where				(We're going) to Malibu Beach.
Why	are	you	going?	(We're going) because we don't have school today.
How				(We're going) by car.
Who *Who* asks about the subject.	is		going with us?	<u>Clara</u> (is going with us).
Who(m) *Whom* asks about the object.	is	she	meeting?	(She's meeting) <u>her friends</u>.

For a review of *who* and *whom*, refer to Unit 9, Focus 5.

Write the question that asks for the underlined information.

1. **Q:** <u>Who is watching television?</u>

   A: <u>Suzy</u> is watching television.

2. **Q:** <u>Who(m) is Regis taking care of tonight?</u>

   A: Regis is taking care of <u>the children.</u>

3. **Q:** _____

   A: Suzy is watching television <u>because she doesn't want to do her homework</u>.

4. **Q:** _____

   A: Robin is meeting <u>her colleagues</u> at the college.

5. **Q:** _____

   A: Robin's thinking <u>that she's lucky to be at work</u>!

6. **Q:** _____

   A: They're eating peanut butter and jelly sandwiches for dinner <u>because Regis's dinner is burnt.</u>

7. **Q:** _____

   A: <u>Regis</u> is watching the children today.

8. **Q:** _____

   A: Regis is taking two aspirin <u>because he has a terrible headache</u>.

9. **Q:** _____

   A: Robin's meeting is taking place <u>at the college.</u>

10. **Q:** _____

    A: Robin is coming home <u>right now.</u>

11. **Q:** _____

    A: Regis is feeling <u>very tired</u> right now.

12. **Q:** _____

    A: <u>The children</u> are making a lot of noise.

Correct the errors in the following sentences.

Example: Is the pizza tasting good?
Does the pizza taste good?

1. The baby and the dog are fight.

2. He's having a new TV.

3. Why you are working today?

4. Are you needing my help?

5. What Robin is thinking?

6. Is she believing him?

7. Right now, he plays cowboy on his father's back.

8. Regis's dinner is not smelling delicious.

9. Where they are going?

10. People no are saving money nowadays.

11. You working hard these days.

12. How you doing today?

Use Your English

ACTIVITY 1 writing/speaking

■ **STEP 1** Your teacher will divide the class into two groups. Group A looks only at the statements in Column A and covers Column B. One student at a time will mime an action. Students in Group B must cover Column A and guess the action. Group B students can ask questions of Group A. Then each Group B student mimes an action from Column B and Group A guesses the action and so on.

COLUMN A	COLUMN B
1. You are opening the lid of a jar. The lid is on very tight.	1. You are reading a very sad story.
2. You are watching a very funny TV show.	2. You are watching your country's soccer team playing in the final game of the World Cup.
3. You are trying to sleep, and a mosquito is bothering you.	3. You are sitting at the bar in a noisy club. At the other side of the bar, there is someone you like. You are trying to get that person's attention.
4. You are crossing a busy street. You are holding a young child by the hand and carrying a bag of groceries in the other hand.	4. You are a dinner guest at a friend's house. Your friend is not a good cook. You don't like the food!
5. You are trying to thread a needle, but you're having trouble finding the eye of the needle.	5. You are cutting up onions to cook dinner.

■ **STEP 2** Make up three situations like those above. Write each situation on a separate piece of paper, and put all the situations in a hat. Every student will then pick a situation and mime it for the others to guess.

ACTIVITY 2 writing

In this unit and Exercise 12, we see that family life is changing in many places. Is family life changing in your home country or in a country that you know? Write sentences expressing habits and things that are generally true or things that are changing for: Mothers Children Grandparents Men Fathers Teenagers Couples Women Discuss your statements in a group or with the whole class.

ACTIVITY 3 listening/speaking

CD Track 14

■ **STEP 1**

You are going to listen to a news report about changing trends in the American family. Before you listen, read the statements below. What do you <u>think</u> is true? Under *Pre-listening*, check *True* or *False* for each statement.

STATEMENTS	PRE-LISTENING		POST-LISTENING	
	TRUE	FALSE	TRUE	FALSE
1. The number of traditional nuclear families is increasing in America.				
2. Hispanic and Asian immigrants are not building traditional nuclear families in the United States.				
3. Americans are only marrying people from their own racial and cultural groups.				
4. The number of children per family is increasing.				
5. More and more unmarried partners are living together.				
6. No children are living with single parents.				
7. More people are choosing to live alone.				

■ **STEP 2**

Now listen to the news report. Under *Post-Listening*, check *True* or *False* according to what you <u>hear</u>. Then compare your answers in Steps 1 and 2. What is surprising about the American family? Discuss this in your group.

ACTIVITY 4  speaking

Work with a partner. Discuss how your lives in the United States today are different from your lives in the countries you come from.

Example: *In my country, I live with my parents. Here, I'm living with three roommates.*

ACTIVITY 5 writing/speaking

STEP 1 Look at the photo on the right. Give this person a name, a nationality, an occupation, an age, and so on. Write a story about this person. What is the woman doing? Where is she? How does she look? What is she thinking about? Why is she there?

STEP 2 Tell the class your story.

ACTIVITY 6 reflection

Work with a partner. Ask each other *yes/no* questions about your experiences learning English in this class. Check *yes* or *no*.

Example: *Are you enjoying this class?*

YES/NO QUESTION	YOU		YOUR PARTNER	
	YES	NO	YES	NO
1. enjoy this class				
2. your English improve				
3. this book help you				
4. make progress in listening and speaking				
5. feel more confident in English				
6. your classmates help you in class				
7. raise your hand more in class				
8. have any specific problems in English				
9. your writing ability improve				
10. your vocabulary increase				
11. use English more				
12. think more about grammar				

ADJECTIVE PHRASES
Another, The Other, Other(s), The Other(s), and Intensifiers

UNIT GOALS

- Understand and know how to use adjective phrases

- Ask questions with *which*

- Understand and use *another, the other, other(s),* and *the other(s)*

- Use intensifiers with adjectives

OPENING TASK
Match Maker

Find the couples. Match one person on the left with a perfect partner on the right by describing both of them. Do not point to the picture.

form   meaning

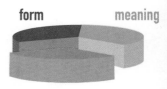

FOCUS 1   Adjective Phrases

EXAMPLES			EXPLANATIONS
Noun	**Adjective Phrase**	**Verb**	
(a) The man	**in the suit**	is a businessman.	Adjective phrases are groups of words that describe nouns.
(b) The diamond ring	**on her finger**	is beautiful.	
The man has a basketball. The man is an athlete.			Adjective phrases combine two sentences.
(c) The man	**with the ball**	is an athlete.	
(d) The **man** with the glasses **is** a businessman.			The verb agrees with the subject, not with the noun in the adjective phrase.
(e) The two **people** on the motorcycle **are** free.			

EXERCISE 1

Underline the subject and the verb in each sentence. Put parentheses around the adjective phrases.

Example: _The man_ (in the suit) _works_ in an office.

1. The man with the bandana drives a motorcycle.
2. The woman with the shopping bags is his girlfriend.
3. The young man with the laptop is a computer programmer.
4. The woman with the dog is in love with the man with the laptop.
5. The gentleman with the briefcase is a businessman.
6. The woman in the dress works for a flower shop.
7. The man with the basketball is physically fit.
8. The woman with the nose ring loves music.
9. The people in the picture on page 253 live in the same apartment building.

These ten people below sit in specific chairs on page 256. Match each person to a chair. Then write a sentence with an adjective phrase to describe where each is sitting. The first one has been done for you.

1.
Megaphone

2.
Bottle

3.
Popcorn

4.
Mirror

5.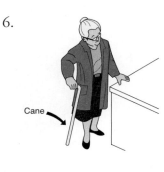
Suitcases

6.
Cane

7.
Crown

8.
Books

9.
Ice Cream Cone

10.
Whistle

a.

b.

c.

d.

e.

f.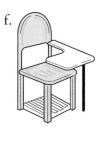

g.

h.

i.

j.

Person	**Chair**	
1. ___1___	___B___	The man with the megaphone sits in chair B.
2. ___2___	_____	
3. ___3___	_____	
4. ___4___	_____	
5. ___5___	_____	
6. ___6___	_____	
7. ___7___	_____	
8. ___8___	_____	
9. ___9___	_____	
10. ___10___	_____	

▌ EXERCISE 3

Combine each of the sentence pairs on the next page into one sentence using an adjective phrase. Then find the person in the picture, and write the number of your sentence on the person. The first one has been done for you.

Kindergarten Chaos

1. The girl has a bow in her hair. She is kicking her partner.
   <u>The girl with the bow in her hair is kicking her partner.</u>

2. The boy has a striped shirt and black pants. He is throwing a paper airplane across the room.

3. The girls are near the window. They are waving to their friends outside.

4. The boy is in a baseball uniform. He is standing on the teacher's desk.

5. The boys are in the back of the room. They are fighting.

6. The boy is in the corner. He is reading.

7. The boy is in the closet. He is crying.

8. The girl has an MP3 player. She is singing.

9. The man has a rope around him. He is the new teacher.

10. The man is in a suit and tie. He is the school principal.

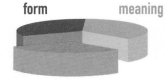

FOCUS 2 | Questions with *Which*

EXAMPLES	EXPLANATIONS
(a) **Which** man is wearing shorts? the athlete (b) **Which** men are conservative? the businessman and the computer programmer	Use *which* when there is a choice between two or more people or things.
(c) **Which** car do they like? They like the small **one**. (d) **Which** shoes do they like? the comfortable **ones**	Substitute the words *one* or *ones* for nouns so you do not repeat the noun.
(e) **Which** restaurant do they want to try? the one with the organic food	You can also use adjective phrases after *one* and *ones*.

EXERCISE 4

Julie's house was robbed. She is very upset, and she is talking to her husband Charles on the phone, describing the damage. Work with a partner. Find the differences between the pictures. One person says Julie's statements. One person is the husband, and asks questions to get more specific information.

Example: **Julie:** *The window is broken.*
Charles: *Which window?*
Julie: *The one over the kitchen sink.*

Before

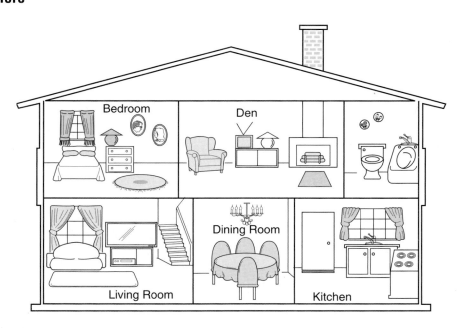

After

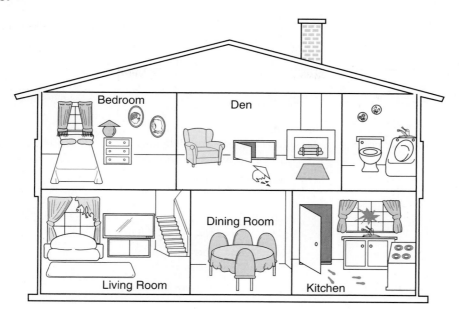

1. The floor is dirty.
2. The curtains are torn.
3. The TV is missing.
4. The door is open.
5. The lamp is broken.
6. The DVD player is missing.
7. The cabinet is empty.
8. The rug is missing.
9. The chandelier is gone.

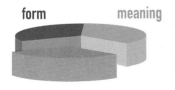

FOCUS 3 | Another, The Other, Other(s), The Other(s)

EXPLANATION	EXAMPLE	MEANING
You can use *another*: before a singular noun	(a) That cookie was so delicious. Can I have **another cookie**?	One more cookie; one more from a group
alone (as a pronoun).	(b) Can I have **another**?	
You can use *other*: before a plural noun	(c) **Child:** There are no more cookies in the box, Mom! **Mom:** Don't worry. There are two **other boxes** in the pantry.	More than one more
alone (as a pronoun).	(d) There are two **others** in the pantry.	
You can use *the other*: before a singular noun	(e) I found one box. Where is **the other box**?	The specific one you spoke about; the last one in the group
alone (as a pronoun) before a plural noun	(f) Where's **the other**? (g) **Sister:** How many more cookies can I have? **Brother:** You can have one more. **The other cookies** are for me!	The specific ones you spoke about; the last ones in a group
alone (as a pronoun)	(h) **The others** are for me!	

▪ EXERCISE 5

Thor is visiting Earth from another planet. Ed Toppil interviews Thor on television. Fill in the blanks with *another, the other, other(s),* or *the other(s).*

Ed: We on Earth are really excited to know there is (1) _____ planet out there, Thor. Many of us know there are (2) _____, but we can't find them. Do you know of any (3) _____ planets?

Thor: Yes, we do. We know two (4) _____: Limbix and Cardiax. I have photos of the people from both of (5) _____ planets.
The Limbix are the ones on the left. The Cardiax are (6) _____ ones. We also now know the planet Earth. We are sure there are (7) _____ out there, but (8) _____ are very far away.

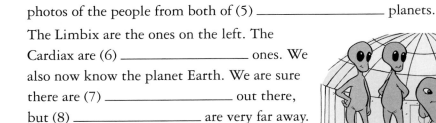

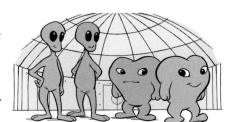

Ed: I am surprised that you speak English so well, Thor. Do the Thoraxes have (9) _____ language, too?

Thor: Yes, of course. We speak Thoracic, but English is a universal language, you know, so we all learn it in school. People on (10) _____ two planets speak English, too!

Ed: So what brings you to Earth?

Thor: Well, Ed, we are looking for (11) _____ intelligent beings in the universe.

Ed: On Earth?!! I don't know if you can find many intelligent beings on Earth, Thor! But we can discuss this at (12) _____ time. Right now, let's stop for a station break.

EXERCISE 6

Thor tours America. Fill in *another, other(s),* or the *other(s).*

1. Thor is in a department store with Ed Toppill.

    Ed: You only have one tie, Thor. You need to buy (a) _____ one.

    Thor: Why?

    Ed: Because Americans are consumers. They like to buy things.

    Thor: But I don't like any (b) _____ ties here.

    Ed: O.K. Look at (c) _____ over there. Maybe you can find (d) _____ one.

2. Thor is in a candy store with a child:

    Thor: Which candy is good here?

    Child: This one is good, but first taste (a) _____ one in the brown and green paper. It's out of this world!

    Thor: Hmmmm, excellent. Is it O.K. to take (b) _____ one?

3. **Soaprah:** So, Thor, tell us about your family. Are you married?

   Thor: Yes. I am, and I have two children. One is a specialist in interplanetary communication and (a) _____ owns a spaceship factory.

   Soaprah: And what does your wife do?

   Thor: My wife is a spaceship pilot.

   Soaprah: What about (b) _____ people on Thorax? What do they do?

   Thor: (c) _____ do different jobs. We have doctors, teachers, artists, and so on. We don't have any tax collectors.

   Soaprah: Are there any (d) _____ professions you don't have?

   Thor: We don't have any lawyers, I'm happy to say.

   Soaprah: That sounds great to me, too!

   Thor: Do you have any (e) _____ questions?

   Soaprah: I have a million (f) _____ questions! But our time is up. It was nice meeting you, Thor. Thanks so much for coming

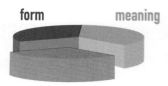
form meaning

FOCUS 4 Intensifiers

Intensifiers are words that make adjectives stronger. The chart below includes some examples of intensifiers.

SUBJECT	*BE*	INTENSIFIER	ADJECTIVE	NOTES
(a) Earth	is	very	beautiful.	
(b) The people on Earth	are	really	interesting.	The word *really* is often used in informal English.
(c) The people on Thorax	are	quite	happy.	
(d) The people on Earth	are	rather/pretty fairly	diverse.	*Pretty* has the same meaning as *rather*, but is very informal.
(e) Thorax	isn't	very really	beautiful.	*Very* and *really* are the only intensifiers we use in negative sentences.

SUBJECT	*BE*	ARTICLE	INTENSIFIER	ADJECTIVE	NOUN
(f) Earth	is	a	very really	special	place.
(g) Thorax	is	a	rather/pretty fairly	small	planet.
(h) Thorax	isn't	a	very really	attractive	place.

SUBJECT	*BE*	INTENSIFIER	ARTICLE	ADJECTIVE	NOUN
(i) Thorax	is	quite	a	small	planet.

Test Thor's knowledge. How many of the objects can Thor (and you) guess?

1. This is fairly long and thin.

    People eat it.

    It is very popular in Italy. What is it? _____

2. This is a liquid.

    People usually drink it hot.

    They like its rather strong, rich smell.

    It's brown. What is it? _____

3. This is an electrical appliance.

    It is quite common in people's homes.

    Sometimes it is very hot.

    You put bread into it. What is it? _____

4. This is very cold.

    It's also pretty hard.

    People put it in drinks on hot days.

    It's quite slippery. What is it? _____

5. This is quite a big metal box.

    It's electrical and pretty practical.

    It's very useful in tall buildings.

    People go inside the box.

    The box goes up and down. What is it? _____

6. This is a very popular piece of plastic.

    With it, we can buy rather expensive things without cash.

    It isn't very big. What is it? _____

7. There are different kinds of candy.

    All of them are good.

    But this one is really special.

    It comes in brown or white.

    It's pretty fattening.

    It's quite delicious. What is it? _____

8. This thing is quite colorful.

    It isn't very common.

    It sometimes follows rainstorms.

    It is quite a beautiful sight. What is it? _____

EXERCISE 8

Ed Toppil continues his interview with Thor. Write an intensifier in each blank. There is more than one possible answer.

Ed: So tell me, Thor, what do you think of our planet?

Thor: Well, Earth is a beautiful planet, but it's (1) _____quite_____ a strange place. Many of your leaders are not doing a (2) _____ good job. Some people on Earth are (3) _____ rich. Others are (4) _____ poor. There can be a (5) _____ big difference between people. On Thorax, we are all equal. Money isn't (6) _____ important. Learning is (7) _____ important. That's why we're visiting Earth. Your knowledge can be (8) _____ useful to us. Also, your art and music are (9) _____ beautiful.

Ed: That's (10) _____ interesting. I'm sure we can learn many (11) _____ useful and exciting things from you, too, Thor.

EXERCISE 9

How necessary or important is each item to you? Give your opinion using intensifiers. Explain your answers.

Example: a cell phone
A cell phone is very important to me. I can call my friends anytime I want.

1. family
2. a life partner
3. designer clothes
4. a university degree
5. children
6. my native language
7. my culture
8. music
9. friends
10. a fancy car

EXERCISE 10

Read the statements and comments. Fill in an intensifier in each blank. Sometimes, there can be more than one possible answer.

Statement	Comment
1. I want to see the movie *Friday the 13th*.	Don't! That's a _____ scary movie!
2. Our teacher is planning an end-of-term party.	That's _____ a nice thing for her to do.
3. How do you like your new digital camera?	It looks easy to use, but it's actually _____ difficult.
4. I like this restaurant very much.	Me, too! This is _____ a delicious dinner.
5. My brother wants to get a motorcycle.	That's not a _____ good idea.
6. He's working in Vietnam.	Really! That's _____ a fascinating place!
7. They have eight children.	Wow! That's a _____ large family.
8. Eric and Tina are doing well in my class.	In mine, too. They're _____ bright students.
9. I'm bored again today.	I'm afraid this is not a _____ exciting vacation.
10. Do you know Newport, Rhode Island?	Oh, yes. The mansions in Newport are _____ big—just like castles.

EXERCISE 11

Correct the errors in the following sentences.

1. The five of us plan to meet at 8:00 tomorrow. I'll tell Mary. You tell the other.

2. This cake is delicious! Can I have other slice?

3. The girl with the brown eyes are my sister.

4. Some of the students are here. Where are the others students?

5. The test wasn't quite difficult.

6. The supermarket is on the another side of the street.

7. There were three books on my desk. One is here. Where are others?

8. I need to go to other school.

9. Please give me the other chance.

10. The exercises in this unit is interesting.

Use Your English

ACTIVITY 1 writing/speaking

- **STEP 1** Write a paragraph (at least six sentences) about your home country or city. Use the topic sentence given below.
  TOPIC SENTENCE:
  My home country/city, _____, is a very wonderful place to visit.

  Examples: *The beaches in the south are very beautiful.*
  The market in the center of the city is always crowded.

- **STEP 2** Now tell the class about your country or city.

ACTIVITY 2 writing/speaking

- **STEP 1** In a group, write sentences about ten students in the class. Use adjective phrases. Use intensifiers when possible. Do not use names.

- **STEP 2** Read your sentences to the class. The class guesses the person you are talking about.

  Examples: *The student from Bogotá is very friendly.*
  The student next to Miyuki is quite a good dancer.
  The student with the big smile is from Ecuador.

ACTIVITY 3 speaking/writing

■ **STEP 1** Check (✔) the adjectives that describe you, and write *very/ quite/rather/pretty/fairly/not very* under **You** in the chart below.

■ **STEP 2** Ask your partner questions to find out which adjectives describe him or her. Then ask questions with how and write *very/quite/rather/pretty/ fairly/not very* under **Your Partner** in the same chart.

Example: **You ask:** *Are you shy?*
Your partner answers: *Yes, I am.*
You ask: *How shy are you?*
Your partner answers: *I'm very shy.*

Adjective	YOU		YOUR PARTNER	
		very really quite rather pretty fairly not very		very really quite rather pretty fairly not very
shy			✔	very
curious				
quiet				
romantic				
outgoing				
old-fashioned				
organized				
jealous				
talkative				
athletic				
adventurous				
sensitive				
caring				
mature				

ACTIVITY 4 writing

Use the information in Activity 3 to write five sentences about you or about your partner using *very/quite/rather/pretty/fairly/not very*.

Example: My partner is a very romantic person. He is pretty old-fashioned, and he is very jealous.

ACTIVITY 5 speaking

Imagine you are starting life on a new planet. Look at the following list of people. Then choose only ten people to move to the new planet. Say how necessary each one is and why. Say why the others are not necessary and why.

Example: A doctor is very necessary because we want to stay healthy.

an actor	an artist	a police officer	a political leader
a scientist	a religious leader	a young man	a young woman
a historian	a writer	a musician	a lawyer
a farmer	a teacher	a journalist	a pilot
a doctor	a mechanic	a computer specialist	a dancer
a military person	a stockbroker	an elderly person	an engineer

ACTIVITY 6 writing/speaking

Guess the object! Write descriptions of objects using intensifiers like those in Exercise 7. Ask your classmates to guess the object.

ACTIVITY **7** listening/speaking

CD Track 15

■ **STEP 1**

Listen to Steffi describing the photograph of her family reunion. Label the picture with the names of the people and their relationship to Steffi.

Steffi's Family Reunion

■ **STEP 2**

Bring in your own photo of a family gathering or a group of friends. Describe the people in the picture to your classmates.

ACTIVITY 8 research on the web

■ **STEP 1** Your partner needs a vacation. Look for a beautiful place for a dream vacation on the Internet. Use a search engine such as Google® or Ask® or Yahoo® and look for photos of three places you think your partner will like. Use keywords such as *vacation*, *beach*, and *island*. Print out the photos.

■ **STEP 2** Show your partner the photos. Ask your partner to choose which vacation place he or she likes the best and (without pointing) to give reasons for his or her choice.

Example: *I like the place with the big beach and pretty trees. The water looks quite warm and blue. The water in the other picture looks quite dark and cold. That beach isn't very attractive.*

ACTIVITY 9 reflection

What is helpful to you as you learn English? Check the things that help you learn English. Discuss why or why not with a partner. Add two of your own.

	YES	NO
1. A school with many computers		
2. A class with other students from my country		
3. Books with audiotapes		
4. A language lab with recording equipment		
5. A reading text with pictures		
6. A teacher with challenging materials		
7. A grammar book with clear explanations and examples		
8. A dictionary with phonetic symbols		
9. Movies with captions		
10. Conversation groups with students from different countries		

UNIT GOALS

- Make affirmative and negative statements with the verb *be* in the past tense

- Ask and answer *yes/no* and *wh*-questions with *be* in the past tense

OPENING TASK

Test Your Memory

Look at the photos of famous people from the past. Make affirmative and negative statements about each person's nationality and occupation. Use the information in the boxes.

NATIONALITY
French
Indian
British
American

OCCUPATION
president
princess
religious leader
civil rights leader
scientist
rock singer

NAME	NATIONALITY	OCCUPATION
1. Martin Luther King, Jr.		
2. The Beatles		
3. Diana		
4. Mahatma Gandhi		
5. Pierre and Marie Curie		
6. George Washington, Thomas Jefferson, Abraham Lincoln, Theodore Roosevelt		

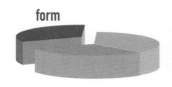
form

FOCUS 1 | Past Tense of *Be*: Affirmative Statements

SUBJECT	VERB	
I	was	
He She It	was	
		famous.
We You They	were	
There	was	a famous actress in that film.
There	were	many political leaders at the meeting.

EXERCISE 1

Use the past tense of *be* to make correct statements about the famous people in the Opening Task.

1. The Beatles _____ a famous British rock group in the 1960s.

2. Mahatma Gandhi _____ a nationalist and Hindu religious leader in India.

3. Marie and Pierre Curie _____ French scientists.

4. George Washington, Thomas Jefferson, Abraham Lincoln, and Theodore Roosevelt _____ presidents of the United States.

5. Martin Luther King, Jr. _____ American civil rights leader.

6. Diana _____ a British princess, the wife of Prince Charles.

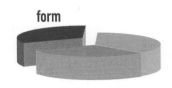

FOCUS 2 — Past Tense of *Be:* Negative Statements

NEGATIVE STATEMENTS			NEGATIVE CONTRACTIONS		
SUBJECT	BE + NOT		SUBJECT	BE + NOT	
I	was not		I	wasn't	
He She It	was not	famous.	He She It	wasn't	famous.
We You They	were not		We You They	weren't	
There	was	no time to eat.	There	wasn't	any time to eat.
There	were	no good restaurants.	There	weren't	any good restaurants.

■ EXERCISE 2

STEP 1 What do you know about Albert Einstein? Read the statements below. Circle (T) for *true* or (F) for *false* for each statement.

1. Albert Einstein was Austrian.   T F
2. As a boy, he wasn't a very good student.   T F
3. He was friendly.   T F
4. He was interested in his classroom subjects.   T F
5. He was a good reader.   T F
6. He was a great thinker.   T F

STEP 2 Read the text below about Albert Einstein. Compare the text to your answers in Step 1. Correct any incorrect sentences in Step 1.

Albert Einstein was born in Germany on March 14, 1879. As a young student, Einstein wasn't very good in school. He wasn't focused in class. His memory was bad. He wasn't a good reader, and spelling was difficult for him. His teachers said he was mentally slow. Other students said young Albert Einstein was unsociable. But everyone was wrong about Einstein. In truth, Albert Einstein was bored in school. The subjects in class weren't interesting to him. Albert Einstein was a scientific genius. By 1920, he was famous around the world. He was the Nobel Prize winner for Physics in 1921.

EXERCISE 3

Read Michael and Carol's views about their trip to Disneyworld, a famous American place. Fill in the blanks with the affirmative or negative of *be* in the simple past. Then role-play the dialogue aloud.

Alice: Oh, hi, Michael. Hi, Carol. How (1) _____ was _____ your trip last week?

Carol: Hi, Alice. Oh, it (2) _____ fun.

Michael: Fun! That vacation (3) _____ (not) fun, it (4) _____ terrible!

Carol: But Michael, how can you say that? I think the children and I (5) _____ very satisfied with our vacation.

Michael: Carol, the weather (6) _____ boiling hot.

Carol: It (7) _____ (not) boiling hot, it (8) _____ very comfortable.

Michael: The food (9) _____ (not) very good . . .

Carol: The food (10) _____ fine, Michael.

Michael: The people (11) _____ rude.

Carol: They (12) _____ (not) rude/They (13) _____ polite and friendly.

Michael: The kids (14) _____ very difficult.

Carol: The kids (15) _____ (not) difficult. They (16) _____ great.

EXERCISE 4

A positive person sees the world in a positive way and believes that good things will happen. A negative person usually sees only the bad things in life. Make sentences using *was/were* for the situations below. These adjectives may help you. Use other adjectives you know.

terrible	ugly	romantic	delicious	beautiful	small	extraordinary	polite
rude	friendly	sunny	fantastic	loud	rainy	ordinary	spacious

SITUATION	A POSITIVE PERSON SAYS:	A NEGATIVE PERSON SAYS:
1. Yesterday evening, you were at a famous restaurant with friends.	a. The place _____. c. The food _____. e. The waiters _____.	b. The place _____. d. The food _____. f. The waiters _____.
2. Last Saturday, you went to a trendy club.	a. The music _____. c. The dance floor _____.	b. The music _____. d. The dance floor _____.
3. Last summer, you were on vacation in Vietnam with your friends.	a. The weather _____. c. The scenery _____. e. The people _____.	b. The weather _____. d. The scenery _____. f. The people _____.

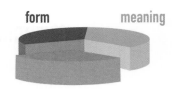

FOCUS 3

Yes/No Questions and Short Answers with *Be* in the Simple Past

form meaning

YES/NO QUESTIONS			SHORT ANSWERS				
VERB	SUBJECT		AFFIRMATIVE			NEGATIVE	
Was	I			you	were.		you were not. you weren't.
Were	you			I	was.		I was not. I wasn't.
Was	he she it	right?	Yes,	he she it	was.	No,	he/she/it was not. he/she/it wasn't.
Were	we you they			you we they	were.		you/we/they were not. you/we/they weren't.
Was there any good food at Disneyworld?			Yes,	there was.		No,	there was not. there wasn't.
Were there long lines at Disneyworld?				there were.			there were not. there weren't.

EXERCISE 5

Detective Furlock Humes is questioning a police officer about a crime. Fill in the blanks with *there* + *be* in the simple past.

Examples: _____Was there_____ a crime last night?

_____Yes, there were_____ several police officers at the house.

Police Officer: The body was here, Detective Humes.

Furlock: (1) _____ a weapon?

Police Officer: Yes, (2) _____ a gun next to the body.

Furlock: (3) _____ any fingerprints on the gun?

Police Officer: No, sir, (4) _____.

Furlock: (5) _____ any motive for this crime?

Police Officer: We don't know, sir.

Furlock: How about witnesses? (6) _____ any witnesses to the crime?

Police Officer: Yes, sir. (7) _____ one witness—a neighbor. She said (8) _____ loud noises in the apartment at midnight.

Furlock: Where is she? Bring her to me . . .

EXERCISE 6

Take turns asking and answering the *yes/no* question about the events below. Give the correct information about the event if it is incorrect.

Example: Margaret Thatcher/the first female Prime Minister of Great Britain.
Was Margaret Thatcher the first female Prime Minister of Great Britain?
Yes, she was.

1. Tom Hanks/the first man to walk on the moon
2. AIDS/a widespread disease in 1949
3. Yugoslavia/a country in 1980
4. Europeans/the first people on the American continent
5. Nelson Mandela/in prison for many years in South Africa
6. The Wright Brothers/the first men to cross the Atlantic Ocean by plane
7. a big earthquake/in Pakistan, in 2005
8. any women/in the Olympic Games in 1920

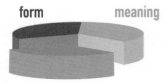

FOCUS 4 — Wh-Questions with *Be*

WH-QUESTION	BE	SUBJECT	ANSWERS
When		JFK's assassination?	November 22, 1963
Where		the assassination?	It was in Dallas, Texas.
Who	was	the assassin?	Lee Harvey Oswald, we think.
What		his motive	There were different theories.
How		the day?	Very sad
Why	were	people sad?	Because Kennedy was a popular president
Whose gun	was	it?	Lee Harvey Oswald's

■ EXERCISE 7

Fill in the *wh*-question word the correct form of *be* to complete each question.

Andrea: (1) _____ you on the day of Kennedy's assassination?

Helene: I was in school. There was an announcement over the loud speaker.

Andrea: (2) _____ you with at the time?

Helene: I was with my friend Patty.

Andrea: (3) _____ school that day?

Helene: It was terrible. We were all very upset and silent.

Andrea: (4) _____ you all silent?

Helene: Because it was hard to belive he was dead.

Andrea: And at home? (5) _____ things at home?

Helene: At home, things were bad. My parents were in shock too.

EXERCISE 8

Look at the photo, and write a *wh*-question for each answer.

1. _____?

   These people were mountain climbers.

2. _____?

   They were in the Himalayas.

3. _____?

   They were there for the adventure and the challenge.

4. _____?

   They were there in 1996.

5. _____?

   The name of the mountain was Mount Everest.

6. _____?

   It was their dream to climb Mt. Everest.

7. _____?

   The trip was a disaster; eight people died on this trip.

Famous Women Information Gap

You look at Chart A below. Your partner looks at Chart B on page A-20. Ask and answer each question about the woman/women. Fill in the information you learn on the chart.

Example: Question 1a: *Who was Anne Frank?*

Answer 1a: *She was a young victim of the Nazis during World War II....*

Chart A

1. Anne Frank	a. who b. why/a victim c. what ... famous for	She was a young victim of the Nazis during World War II.
2. Susan B. Anthony & Elizabeth Cady Stanton		d. two important "suffragists" in the United States e. their fight for voting and equal rights for women f. in the late 1800's and early 1900's
3. Amelia Earhart	g. who h. what/famous for i. when/her flight	
4. Indira Gandhi		j. what/famous for k. whose daughter l. what/her father/famous for

EXERCISE 10

Correct the errors in the following sentences.

1. Do was Mahatma Gandhi a religious leader in India?

2. The Beatles wasn't fashion designers.

3. Was hot the weather at Disneyworld last week?

4. Where the earthquake was in 2005?

5. Why the people were on Mount Everest?

6. Was good the service at the restaurant?

7. No was any good restaurants in Disneyworld.

8. How it was the trip to Disneyworld?

EXERCISE 11

What are your earliest childhood memories? Think about some of your favorite things from your childhood. Work in a group of four. Take turns asking questions about your favorite things below.

Example: *When you were a child, what was your favorite food?*
When you were a child, who was your favorite relative?

1. food

2. relative

3. holiday

4. hobby

5. toy/game

6. TV program

7. teacher

8. friend

9. birthday

10. day of the week

11. subject in school

Use Your English

ACTIVITY 1 speaking

Work with a partner. Ask your partner the questions below and your own questions to find out about a place that is special to him or her.

Questions: *What place was special to you? When were you there?*
Why were you there? What was special about this place?
How was the weather? Were the people friendly? How was the food?

ACTIVITY 2 speaking/writing

With the information from Activity 1, write a paragraph about your partner's special place. Then, tell the class something interesting about your partner's special place.

Example: *Last summer, my partner was in Greece. She was there with her friend. Greece was very beautiful and interesting.*

ACTIVITY 3 speaking

Work in a group.

■ **STEP 1**   Write each of the dates/times below on a separate piece of paper. Mix all the papers together.

On December 31, 1999	In the 90's	In the summer of 2001
On September 11, 2001	In the 80's	In the fall of 2002
On December 26, 2004	In the 70's	On my birthday in 2005

■ **STEP 2**   Pick a piece of paper, and say something about your life at that time and your life now. Take turns with the classmates in your group.

Example: *In the 90's, I was a doctor in the Philippines, but now I am an ESL student in the United States.*

ACTIVITY **4**   research on the web

■ **STEP 1**   Go to the Internet to find out information about the famous people listed below. Use a search engine such as Google®, Yahoo®, or Ask® and enter each name in the search box. Other useful sites to find this information is www.answers.com or Wikipedia.com. Find out what the person was famous for and where the person was from. Write the information in the chart.

FAMOUS PERSON	FAMOUS FOR	COUNTRY
Che Guevara		
Sigmund Freud		
Jonas Salk		
Louis Armstrong		
Helen Keller		
Charlie Chaplin		
Frank Sinatra		
Marilyn Monroe		
Lucille Ball		
Ho Chi Minh		
Mother Teresa		
Pablo Picasso		
Winston Churchill		
Abbott and Costello		

■ **STEP 2** Write the names of the famous people from the chart above on large index cards. Place the cards face down on the desk. Each student chooses a card and tapes the card to another student's back. Each student asks *yes/no* questions to try to guess who he/she was. Use these clues to help you:

Nationality	*Was I American? Latin American? European? Asian?*
Gender	*Was I a man? A woman?*
Occupation	*Was I an actor/actress? A doctor? A political activist?*

ACTIVITY 5 listening/speaking

Listen to the story of the Titanic. Write an answer to each question below.

CD Track 16

1. Who were the passengers on the Titanic?
2. How many people were there on the ship?
3. How was the weather the night of the accident?
4. What was the cause of the accident?
5. How cold was the water?
6. Why were there many deaths?

ACTIVITY 6 reflection

Compare yourself as a language learner from the time when you started learning English to now. Are you a better language learner now? Write your reflection and then discuss this with a partner.

Example: *I think I'm a better language learner now. Before I was afraid to speak English. Now I'm confident. . . . .*

UNIT GOALS

- Make affirmative and negative statements with regular and irregular simple past tense verbs

- Know how to spell and pronounce regular past tense verbs

- Understand the meaning and position of past time expressions

- Ask and answer *yes/no* and *wh*-questions in the past tense

OPENING TASK

Solve the Mystery: Who Took Ms. Kudo's Flash Drive?

■ STEP 1

Read the mystery.

For almost everyone at the college, Ms. Kudo was the best ESL teacher. She won many awards for her excellent teaching and materials. She taught her students about language, culture, and history. She discussed film and television in class. She helped the students do Internet research in the computer lab. They wrote every day in her class. They went on trips together. The students enjoyed her classes and really learned. Everyone liked her—except for one student, Leo, and one of the teachers, Mr. Dim.

Leo was not a serious ESL student. He made no effort to learn, so Ms. Kudo refused to have him in her class. The Director put Leo in Mr. Dim's class, but Leo wasn't happy there. Leo blamed Ms. Kudo for his unhappiness. The teacher, Mr. Dim, disliked Ms. Kudo.

He felt jealous of all Ms. Kudo's teaching awards. Mr. Dim felt he was a good teacher, but nobody noticed him.

Ms. Kudo saved all her ideas and teaching materials on her flash drive. She kept her flash drive in her school bag. Everyone knew that. On the first day of the new semester, Ms. Kudo's flash drive disappeared. She looked everywhere, but she didn't find it. Instead, she found a type-written letter.

The letter said:

> Ms. Kudo:
>
> Today, I very sad. I no can stay in English Language Center because no am important in here. Always Ms. Kudo, Ms. Kudo. And me? What I am? What I can do? How I continue to teach here? I also teach good. No is easy for me here. I take your flash drive because I have angry. Please understand my . . .

Ms. Kudo reported the theft to the Director. She gave the Director the letter.

■ STEP 2

Read the sentences and check *True* or *False*.

	TRUE	FALSE
1. Someone wanted to hurt Ms. Kudo.		
2. Ms. Kudo's students didn't like her.		
3. Leo was happy in Mr. Dim's class.		
4. Ms. Kudo wanted Leo in her class.		
5. Mr. Dim felt jealous of Ms. Kudo.		
6. Leo blamed himself for being unhappy.		
7. The note was well written.		

■ STEP 3

Who took Ms. Kudo's flash drive? How do you know? Discuss your answers with the class.

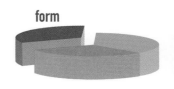

FOCUS 1 Forming and Spelling Regular Past Tense Verbs

SUBJECT	BASE FORM + -*ED*
I He She It We You They	started three years ago.

Regular verbs can change spelling in the simple past tense.

IF THE VERB ENDS IN:	SPELLING RULE
(a) a consonant want need	Add *ed* wanted needed
(b) a vowel + *y* enjoy play	Add *ed* enjoyed played
(c) a consonant + *e* like smile	Add *d* liked smiled

IF THE VERB ENDS IN:	SPELLING RULE
(d) a consonant + *y* **study** **worry**	Change *y* to *i*, add *ed* **studied** **worried**
(e) consonant + vowel + consonant (one syllable verbs) **stop** **drop**	Double the consonant, add *ed* **stopped** **dropped**
(f) *x* or *w* (one syllable verbs) **show** **fix**	Do not double the consonant, add *ed* **showed** **fixed**
(g) two-syllable verbs with the stress on the last syllable **ocCUR** **preFER**	Double the consonant, add *ed* **occurred** **preferred**
(h) two-syllable verbs with the stress on the first syllable **LISten** **VISit**	Do not double the consonant, add *ed* **listened** **visited**

EXERCISE 1

Go back to the Opening Task on pages 286–287, and underline all the **regular** past tense verbs in the mystery story and letter.

Example: *She* _____discussed_____ *film and television in class.*

EXERCISE 2

Fill in the blanks with the past tense of the verbs.

1. Ms. Kudo _____ (enjoy) teaching.

2. Ms. Kudo _____ (use) film and television in class.

3. She _____ (help) her students do research on the Internet.

4. The students _____ (study) new ideas and vocabulary.

5. They _____ (learn) about culture and history.

6. They _____ (discuss) many topics in class.

7. The students _____ (work) on group projects.

8. Many students _____ (register) for her class every semester.

9. Ms. Kudo _____ (receive) many awards for her excellent teaching.

10. Almost everyone _____ (like) Ms. Kudo.

11. One day, a crime _____ (occur) at the English Language Center.

12. Ms. Kudo's flash drive _____ (disappear).

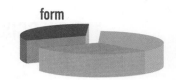

form

FOCUS 2 — Pronunciation of the *ed* Ending

VERB END	EXAMPLES	
Group I After voiceless sounds,* the final *ed* is pronounced /t/.	**/t/**	
	asked	*washed*
	kissed	*sniffed*
	stopped	*matched*
Group II After voiced sounds,** the final *ed* is pronounced /d/.	**/d/**	
	robbed	*waved*
	killed	*rained*
	played	*begged*
	gazed	*harmed*
	shared	
Group III After /t/ and /d/, the final *ed* is pronounced /Id/.	**/Id/**	
	pointed	*needed*
	wanted	*ended*
	waited	*added*

*When you make a **voiceless** sound, your vocal chords don't vibrate. (Put your hand on your throat. Say the sound. If you don't feel a vibration, the sound is voiceless.)

** When you make a **voiced** sound, your vocal chords vibrate. (Put your hand on your throat. Say the sound. If you feel a vibration, the sound is voiced.)

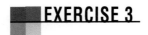

EXERCISE 3

STEP 1   Put each verb in the simple past, and read each sentence aloud. Check the column that shows the pronunciation of each verb.

Bookworm Benny was an excellent student.	/T/	/D/	/ID/
1. Teachers always ____liked____ (like) Bookworm Benny.			
2. He _____ (work) hard in school.			
3. He always _____ (finish) his work first.			
4. The teacher always _____ (call) on him.			
5. He always _____ (answer) questions correctly.			
6. He _____ (remember) all his lessons.			
7. He never _____ (talk) out of turn.			
8. The other students _____ (hate) Benny.			
9. One day, they _____ (decide) to get him into trouble.			
10. They _____ (roll) a piece of paper into a ball.			
11. They _____ (wait) for the teacher to turn his back.			
12. They threw the paper ball at the teacher. It _____ (land) on the teacher's head.			
13. The teacher was really angry. He _____ (yell) at the class.			
14. "Who did that?" he _____ (ask).			
15. All the students _____ (point) to Benny.			
16. But the teacher _____ (trust) Benny.			
17. The teacher _____ (punish) the other students.			

STEP 2   The pictures about Bookworm Benny on the next page are not in the correct order. Number the pictures in the correct order. Then retell Bookworm Benny's story using only the pictures.

a. Number _____   b. Number _____   c. Number _____

d. Number _____   e. Number _____

EXERCISE 4

This exercise contains the solution to the Opening Task mystery. Fill in the blanks with the past tense of the verbs shown in the box below.

look	remember	call	type	learn
realize	confess	want	discuss	lock
notice	remove	complain		

When the Director of the English Language Center (1) _____learned_____ about Ms. Kudo's flash drive, she was surprised. She (2) _____ to understand this crime.

   To solve the mystery, the Director (3) _____ herself in her office to think. She (4) _____ that Mr. Dim was jealous of Ms. Kudo. She also (5) _____ a conversation with Leo about moving to Mr. Dim's class. Leo (6) _____ about Mr. Dim's class. Then, the Director (7) _____ at the note again. She (8) _____ all the grammar mistakes! The Director (9) _____ Leo to her office.

   She (10) _____ the problem with him. Finally, Leo (11) _____ to the crime. Leo said, "I (12) _____ the note. I (13) _____ the flash drive from her bag."

(See Exercise 5 on page 297 for a possible ending)

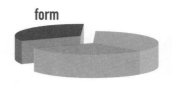

FOCUS 3 | Irregular Past-Tense Verbs: Affirmative Statements

Many verbs in the past tense are irregular. They do not have the *ed* form.

SUBJECT	VERB	
I He She It We You They	went	to Miami last year.

You can learn irregular past tense forms in groups.

BASE FORM	SIMPLE PAST
/I/ sound	/æ/ sound
begin	began
drink	drank
ring	rang
sing	sang
sink	sank
swim	swam

BASE FORM	SIMPLE PAST
	ought/aught
buy	bought
bring	brought
catch	caught
fight	fought
teach	taught
think	thought

BASE FORM	SIMPLE PAST
	Base form and past-tense forms are the same.
cost	cost
cut	cut
hit	hit
hurt	hurt
put	put
quit	quit
shut	shut
let	let
-ow	**-ew**
blow	blew
grow	grew
know	knew
throw	threw
/iy/ sound	**/ɛ/ sound**
feed	fed
feel	felt
keep	kept
lead	led
leave	left
meet	met
read	read
sleep	slept
-d	**-t**
lend	lent
send	sent
spend	spent
bend	bent
build	built

BASE FORM	SIMPLE PAST
	Change of vowel
become	became
come	came
dig	dug
draw	drew
fall	fell
forget	forgot
forgive	forgave
get	got
give	gave
hold	held
hang	hung
run	ran
sit	sat
win	won
	/o/ sound
break	broke
choose	chose
sell	sold
tell	told
speak	spoke
steal	stole
drive	drove
ride	rode
wake	woke
write	wrote

BASE FORM	SIMPLE PAST
	Other These verbs have unique changes in the past form.
be	was
bite	bit
do	did
eat	ate
find	found
fly	flew
go	went
have	had
hear	heard
hide	hid
lose	lost
make	made
pay	paid
say	said
see	saw
shake	shook
shoot	shot
stand	stood
take	took
tear	tore
understand	understood
wear	wore

(See Appendix 8 on page A-8 for an alphabetical list of common irregular past tense verbs.)

EXERCISE 5

Here is one possible ending to the mystery story. Fill in the correct simple past tense verb forms.

In the end, the Director (1) _____ (give) Leo a second chance. True, Leo (2) _____ (hurt) everyone, but the Director (3) _____ (feel) Leo was able to change. Ms. Kudo (4) _____ (forgive) Leo. She (5) _____ (take) Leo into her class. She (6) _____ (spend) many afternoons in school with Leo. Leo (7) _____ (become) more serious. His English (8) _____ (get) better.

   The Director also (9) _____ (speak) to Mr. Dim about his teaching. She (10) _____ (tell) Mr. Dim to visit Ms. Kudo's class. Mr.Dim (11) _____ (sit) in Ms. Kudo's class many times. As a result, Mr. Dim (12) _____ (begin) to teach differently.

EXERCISE 6

Liisa and Katja are from Finland. They had a **dream vacation** in New York last fall. Fill in the blanks with the simple past tense of the verbs in parentheses.

1. Liisa and Katja _____ flew _____ (fly) to New York on Sunday, November 4.

2. They _____ (find) many interesting things to do in the city.

3. They _____ (eat) great food every day.

4. They _____ (go) to the Statue of Liberty.

5. They _____ (take) a ferry to the Immigration Museum at Ellis Island.

6. They _____ (stand) in the middle of Times Square.

7. They _____ (spend) an evening at a jazz club.

8. Liisa _____ (buy) gifts for her friends in Finland.

9. They _____ (see) an exhibit at the Museum of Modern Art.

10. They _____ (meet) a nice woman at the museum.

11. They _____ (speak) English with her all afternoon.

12. They _____ (think) New York was a beautiful, friendly city.

EXERCISE 7

Monique and Daniel are from France. Their vacation in New York was a **nightmare**. Fill in the blanks with the simple past tense of the verbs in parentheses.

1. On Sunday, November 4, Monique and Daniel's flight to New York was late, so they _____sat_____ (sit) in the airport in Paris for four hours.

2. The airline company _____ (lose) all their luggage, so on Monday they _____ (go) shopping for new clothes.

3. On Tuesday, they _____ (get) stuck in the subway when their train _____ (break) down.

4. On Wednesday, they _____ (pay) ninety dollars to rent a car, and _____ (drive) to the Aquarium.

5. They _____ (leave) the car on the street and _____ (get) a $115.00 parking ticket!

6. Monique _____ (lose) her digital camera in the Aquarium.

7. On Thursday, they _____ (buy) a new camera downtown.

8. On Friday, they _____ (go) ice skating at Rockefeller Center. Monique had the new camera around her neck.

9. Monique _____ (fall) on the ice _____ (hurt) her knee.

10. She _____ (break) her new camera.

11. Monique was wet and frozen, so she _____ (catch) a cold.

12. On Saturday, there _____ (be) a snowstorm; the city _____ (be) silent and still. There _____ (be) no transportation.

13. All the theaters _____ (shut) their doors, so Monique and Daniel missed their night at a Broadway show.

14. On Sunday, they _____ (take) a taxi to the airport and finally _____ (leave) for home.

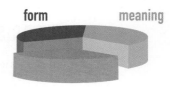

FOCUS 4   Time Expressions in the Past

Time expressions tell us when the action occurred in the past.

TIME EXPRESSION	EXAMPLES	EXPLANATIONS
in 1998 on Sunday at 6:00 the day before yesterday	(a) **On Sunday,** they flew to New York.	Time expressions can come at the beginning or at the end of a sentence.
an hour **ago** two days **ago** six months **ago** a year **ago**	(b) Liisa and Kate went to Spain **two years ago.**	
yesterday morning **yesterday** afternoon **yesterday** evening	(c) **Yesterday morning,** a flash drive disappeared from the Center.	Use a comma after the time expression if it is at the beginning of the sentence.
last night **last** week **last** month **last** year **last** summer	(d) We took two summer school classes last summer.	Do not use a comma before a time expression at the end of a sentence.

EXERCISE 8

On Tuesday, November 13th, Monique and Daniel talked to their friend Colette about their trip. Complete the sentences with time expressions.

Colette: Hi, guys! When did you get back?

Monique: We got home (1) _____ 8:00 yesterday morning.

Colette: So, how was your trip?

Daniel: Well, let's say that (2) _____ week was a week to remember! Our plane arrived in New York four hours late (3) _____ Sunday. Today's Tuesday, right? Well, exactly a week (4) _____, we got stuck in the New York City subway for two hours! Then, (5) _____ Wednesday, we got a parking ticket for $115.00. What else? Oh, (6) _____ Thursday, we bought a new digital camera and Monique accidentally broke it. The day we left there was a big snowstorm.

Monique: As you can see, (7) _____ week was difficult! We were happy to come home (8) _____ Sunday. Our trip to New York four years (9) _____ was much better!

Make true statements about yourself. Use each of the time expressions below.

Example: Six months ago, _____ I took a trip to Mexico _____.

1. Two months ago, _____.
2. In 2001, _____.
3. Last year, _____.
4. Last summer, _____.
5. Two days ago, _____.
6. On Sunday, _____.
7. The day before yesterday, _____.
8. Yesterday morning, _____.
9. At six o'clock this morning, _____.
10. An hour ago, _____.

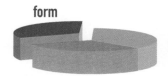

form

FOCUS 5	Past Tense: Negative Statements

SUBJECT	DID + NOT/DIDN'T	BASE FORM OF VERB
I He She It We You They	did not didn't	work.

EXERCISE 10

Make affirmative or negative statements aloud about the people in this unit.

Example: the teacher/like Benny
The teacher liked Benny
the teacher/get angry at Benny.
The teacher didn't get angry at Benny

1. The other students/like Bookworm Benny

2. The teacher/trust Benny

3. The students/try to get Benny into trouble

4. The students' plan for Benny/succeed

5. Liisa and Katja/lose their luggage

6. Liisa's digital camera/break

7. Liisa and Katja/get stuck on the subway

8. Liisa and Katja/enjoy their vacation in New York

9. Leo/notice the grammar mistakes in his note

10. Mr. Dim/ feel jealous of Ms. Kudo

11. Leo/steal Ms. Kudo's flash drive

12. The Director/punish Leo

13. Monique and Daniel/spend an evening at a jazz club

14. Monique and Daniel/visit the Statue of Liberty

15. Monique and Daniel/enjoy their vacation in New York

form

FOCUS 6   Past Tense: *Yes/No* Questions and Short Answers

Yes/No Questions

DID	SUBJECT	BASE FORM OF THE VERB	
Did	I he she we you they	visit	New York last year?

Short Answers

AFFIRMATIVE			NEGATIVE		
Yes,	I he she we you they	did.	No,	I he she we you they	did not. didn't.

EXERCISE 11

Ask a partner *yes/no* questions about Ms. Kudo's story.

Example: understand the mystery
You: *Did you understand the mystery?*
Your partner: *Yes, I did.*

1. like the mystery story
2. enjoy being a detective
3. think Mr. Dim was the thief
4. guess that Leo was the thief

5. find the grammar mistakes in Leo's note
6. correct the mistakes in the note
7. agree with the Director's decision
8. want the Director to punish Leo?

EXERCISE 12

Look at the cartoons about Jinxed Jerry, a man with very bad luck. He went on a two-week Caribbean cruise last winter and there was a hurricane at sea.

STEP 1 Ask a partner *yes/no* questions with the words below. The pictures can help you answer the questions.

Example: Jerry/go on a cruise last winter
You: *Did Jerry go on a cruise last winter?*
Your partner: *Yes, he did.*

1. Jerry's ship/get to the Caribbean
2. Jerry/know how to swim
3. Jerry/die
4. he/find an island
5. he/meet anyone on the island
6. the island/have stores
7. he/have enough food
8. he/write postcards home
9. he/make tools
10. he/build a good boat

STEP 2 Remember, Jerry has very bad luck. Ask each other *yes/no* questions and guess the end of the story.

11. Jerry's luck/change
12. a helicopter/find Jerry
13. Jerry/find his way back home
14. the story/have a happy ending
15. Jerry/ever take another cruise again

See the Appendix for the conclusion to Exercise 12 (page A-22).

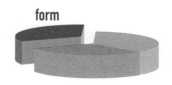

FOCUS 7 | Past Tense: *Wh*-Questions

WH-WORD	DID	SUBJECT	BASE FORM OF VERB	ANSWERS
What		I	do last summer?	You went to Paris.
When		you	make plans?	(I made plans) last month.
Where		he	go last summer?	(He went) to Scotland.
Why		the ship	sink?	(It sank) because there was a storm.
How	did	she	get to Paris?	(She got there) by plane.
How long		they	stay in New York?	(They stayed there for) two weeks.
How long ago		you	visit Alaska?	(I visited Alaska) ten years ago.
Who(m)		Liisa and Katja	meet in New York?	(They met) a friendly woman.

WH-WORD AS SUBJECT	PAST TENSE VERB	ANSWERS
What	happened to Jerry's ship?	It sank.
Who	had a terrible vacation?	Monique and Daniel (did).

EXERCISE 13

Write *wh*-questions about Jerry. Then ask your partner the questions. Your partner gives an answer or says "I don't know."

Example: Jerry/eat on the island?
Q: *What did Jerry eat on the island?*
A: *(He ate) fruit from the trees and fish from the sea.*

1. Jerry/want to go on vacation

   Q: Where _____?

   A: _____

2. Jerry/go on vacation

   Q: When _____?

   A: _____

3. Jerry/leave home

   Q: How long ago _____?

   A: _____

4. Jerry's ship/sink

   Q: Why _____?

   A: _____

5. Jerry/do after the ship sank

   Q: What _____?

   A: _____

6. Jerry/meet on the island

   Q: Who(m) _____?

   A: _____

7. Jerry/build the boat

   Q: How _____?

   A: _____

8. Jerry/put on the boat

   Q: What _____?

   A: _____

9. Jerry/feel when he finished the boat

   Q: How _____?

   A: _____

10. the story end (in your opinion)

   Q: How _____?

   A: _____

STEP 1   Make questions that ask for the underlined information. Use *who*, *whom*, *why*, *how* or *what*.

Example: Q: *Who won awards for teaching?*   A: *Ms. Kudo won awards.*

1. Q: _____?
   A: The Director solved the mystery <u>by reading the note carefully</u>.

2. Q: _____?
   A: <u>Leo</u> lied. <u>Mr. Dim</u> didn't lie.

3. Q: _____?
   A: Leo stole <u>Ms. Kudo's flash drive</u>.

4. Q: _____?
   A: Leo hurt <u>everyone: Ms. Kudo, Mr. Dim, the Director, and himself</u>.

5. Q: _____?
   A: <u>The Director</u> made the decision about Leo.

6. Q: _____?
   A: The Director gave Leo a second chance <u>because she believed Leo was able to change</u>.

7. Q: _____?
   A: The moral of the story was <u>"crime doesn't pay."</u>

STEP 2   What did you think of the Director's decision? Check (a) or (b), and give reasons for your answers in writing. Discuss with the class.

_____ a. I liked the Director's decision.   _____ b. I disagreed with the Director's decision.

EXERCISE 15

Correct the errors in the following sentences.

1. This morning, I waked up early.
2. I saw him yesterday night.
3. Leo didn't felt happy.
4. They don't met the Mayor of New York last week.
5. What Leo wanted?
6. Leo didn't noticed his mistakes.
7. Who did signed the note?

8. What did the Director?

9. What did happened to Leo?

10. Where Liisa and Katja went on vacation?

11. Who did go with Liisa to New York?

12. How Jerry built a boat?

13. They no had dinner in a Greek restaurant.

14. Whom did trust the teacher in the Bookworm Benny story?

15. Doina escaped from Romania before a long time.

EXERCISE 16

Information Gap. This is a true story about a very special woman named Doina. Work with a partner. You look at Text A below. Your partner looks at Text B on page A-21. Take turns asking questions to get the information in the blanks.

Example: **Your partner:** *(Look at Text B)*   *1. Where did Doina grow up?*
        You: *(Look at Text A)*   *1. She grew up in Romania.*

TEXT A:

1. Doina grew up in Romania.

2. She married _____ (who/m).

3. She had a daughter.

4. Doina was unhappy because she was against the government in Romania.

5. She thought of _____ (what) every day.

6. She taught her daughter how to swim.

7. On October 9, 1988, she and her daughter swam across the Danube River. They swam to _____ (where).

8. The police caught them.

9. Doina and her daughter went _____ (where).

10. They tried to escape several months later.

11. Finally, they left Romania _____ (how).

12. They flew to New York in 1989.

13. Doina went to school _____ (why).

14. She wrote the story of her escape from Romania in her ESL class.

Use Your English

ACTIVITY 1 speaking

■ **STEP 1**   Work in groups. One person in the group thinks of a famous person from the past.

■ **STEP 2**   The others in the group can ask up to twenty *yes/no* questions to guess who the person is. After twenty questions, the group loses if they haven't guessed.

Example: *Did this person sing?*
Did this person live in North America?
Was this person a woman?

ACTIVITY 2 speaking

■ **STEP 1**   **Who is telling the truth?** Work in groups of three. Each student tells a **true personal story.** The group chooses one of the stories. Then the other two students learn as much as they can about that story.

■ **STEP 2**   The first group sits in front of the room. Each of the three students tells the same beginning of the story to the class. The rest of the class asks the three students questions to find out who is telling the truth.

Example: **Student 1, 2 and 3 each says:** *When I was ten years old, I went on a long trip.*
The class asks each person a question: *Student 1, where did you go? Student 2, who(m) did you go with? Student 3, why did you go there?*

■ **STEP 3**   The class takes a vote on who(m) they think is telling the truth. Finally, the student with the true story stands up.

ACTIVITY 3 writing/speaking

Write your own ending for the story about Jinxed Jerry. Compare your ending
with your classmates'. Who has the best ending? When you are finished, look at
the cartoons that tell the end of Jerry's story on page A-22. Discuss how your
ending compares with the ending in the cartoon.

ACTIVITY 4 speaking

Interview a partner about a past vacation. Ask as many *wh*-questions as you can.
Report back to the class about your partner's trip.

Example: *Where did you go?*   *How long did you stay?*
              When did you go?   *With whom did you go?*
              How did you get there?   *Why did you go there?*
              What did you do there?

ACTIVITY 5 listening/speaking

CD Track 17

■ **STEP 1**   Listen to another possible ending of the Opening Task mystery
              story.

■ **STEP 2**   How is this ending different from the ending in Exercise 5
              (page 297)? In which ending did the Director make the best
              decision? Why?

ACTIVITY 6 speaking

Jeopardy Game. Your teacher will choose one student to be the host. Only the host can look at the complete game board (page A-21). The rest of the class will be divided into two teams. Team 1 chooses a category and an amount of money from the blank game board below. The host reads the answer. Team 1 has one minute to ask a correct question. If Team 1 can't, Team 2 gets a chance to ask a question. There may be more than one correct question for each answer. Your teacher decides on the "correctness" of the question and answer. The team with the most money wins.

Example: **Team 1 chooses:** *"People" for ten dollars.*
Host reads: *Ms. Kudo*
Team 1 asks: *Who forgave Leo?*

Game Board

$$$	CATEGORY 1 PEOPLE	CATEGORY 2 *WH*-QUESTIONS	CATEGORY 3 *YES/NO* QUESTIONS
$10			
$20			
$30			
$40			
$50			

ACTIVITY 7 writing/speaking

The stories in this unit are about unlucky things that happen to people and how people escape from difficult situations. Think about a time when something unlucky happened to you or when you escaped from a difficult situation. Write your story, and then tell the class what happened. Your classmates can ask you questions.

ACTIVITY 8   research on the web

Sir Ernest Shackleton was a famous explorer. In 1914, Shackleton left London with his crew to explore Antarctica on his ship *Endurance*. He and his ship disappeared a few months later. They finally returned to London two years later. What happened?

■ **STEP 1**   Write a list of *wh*-questions about Shackleton and *Endurance*.

■ **STEP 2**   Search the Internet for answers to your *wh*-questions. Use an online information source such as Ask.com or Wikipedia.com. Enter keyword groups like these: *Shackleton; Shackleton* and *biography; Shackleton* and *time line.* Share your answers with the class.

ACTIVITY 9   reflection

Think of the ESL/EFL classrooms in your own experience. What kind of classroom language learning activities did you do/not do in your country? What kind of activities did the students in Ms. Kudo's class do? What classroom activities did you do/not do in this country? Which activities did you find most useful? Discuss this as a class.

REFLEXIVE PRONOUNS, RECIPROCAL PRONOUN: *EACH OTHER*

UNIT GOALS

- Use reflexive pronouns correctly

- Know which verbs are commonly used with reflexive pronouns

- Know how to use *each other*

OPENING TASK
Advice Columns

■ STEP 1

Read the letters to "Dear Darcy" in Part A. Match each one to a "Letter of Advice" in Part B. Fill in the name of the person who wrote each letter in the blanks in Part B.

PART A: Letters to Dear Darcy

Dear Darcy,

My wife and I never go out anymore. We have a new baby, and my wife doesn't want to get a babysitter. I need a social life. I'm starting to talk to myself! Can you help me?
—*Bored in Boston*

Dear Darcy,

I'm married and have two children. I'm trying to be a superwoman. I work outside the home. I also do all of the housework, the shopping, and the cleaning. I help my children with their schoolwork. I never have time for myself. I am tired and unhappy. Please help!
—*Supermom in Seattle*

Dear Darcy,

My mom and dad got divorced last month. They fought with each other a lot, and finally, my dad moved out. Maybe I wasn't a good daughter to them. Maybe the breakup was my fault. I can't forgive myself.
—*Guilty in Gainesville*

PART B: Letters of Advice

a. Dear _____,
Don't blame yourself. You did not cause these problems. Your parents need to learn to talk to each other.

b. Dear _____,
You need to explain how you feel to her. Tell her you want to go out once a week. Life is short. Find a babysitter. Go out and enjoy yourselves!

c. Dear_____,
You need to make time for yourself. Go out with your friends. Do yourself a favor and join a gym. Take care of yourself, too. Buy yourself something special.

■ STEP 2

Read the letter from *Lonely in Los Angeles.* Then read Darcy's response and circle the correct pronouns.

Dear Darcy,

I'm a rather shy and lonely international student in high school. I'm doing well in school, but I don't have many friends. The students in my classes always talk to each other, but they never include me. I don't go out. I don't enjoy myself. I don't even like myself very much anymore.

—*Lonely in Los Angeles*

Dear Lonely in Los Angeles,

Remember, the teenage years are difficult. At 16, many teenagers don't like (1) (they/them/themselves). You're doing well in school. Be proud of (2) (you/yourself). Try to like (3) (you/yourself) first. Then others will like (4) (you/yourself). Teenagers need (5) (each other/themselves). Force (6) (you/yourself) to open up to others. Relax and try to enjoy (7) (you/yourself).

—*Darcy*

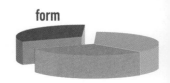

FOCUS 1   Reflexive Pronouns

Use a reflexive pronoun when the subject and object are the same.

Example: Sara bought **herself** a new car.
NOT: Sara bought Sara a new car.

EXAMPLES	REFLEXIVE PRONOUNS
(a) I bought **myself** a new car.	*myself*
(b) Look at **yourself** in the mirror.	*yourself*
(c) He doesn't take care of **himself**.	*himself*
(d) She blames **herself** for the accident.	*herself*
(e) A cat licks **itself** to keep clean.	*itself*
(f) We enjoyed **ourselves** at the theater.	*ourselves*
(g) Help **yourselves** to some food.	*yourselves*
(h) Babies can't feed **themselves**.	*themselves*

EXERCISE 1

Go back to Step 1 in the Opening Task on page 312. Underline all the reflexive pronouns and circle the subjects.

Example: (I) never have time for <u>myself</u>.

EXERCISE 2

Fill in each blank with a reflexive pronoun.

Example: I lost my wallet yesterday, and I just wanted to kick _____myself_____.

1.   **Mary:** Do you sometimes talk to (a) _____?

     Bill: Well, yes. I talk to (b) _____ pretty often. I always give
     (c) _____ advice!

2.   **Monica:** Thanks for such a lovely evening. We really enjoyed
     (a) _____.

     Gloria: Well, thanks for coming. And the children were just wonderful. They
     really behaved (b) _____ all evening. I hope you can
     come back soon.

3.   **Jane:** I can't believe my bird flew out the window! It's my fault. I forgot to close
     the birdcage.

     Margaret: Don't blame _____. He's probably happier now. He's free!

4. **Cynthia:** What's the matter with Bobby's leg?

   Enrique: He hurt _____ at the soccer game last night.

5. **Jason:** My girlfriend Judy really knows how to take care of _____. She eats well, exercises regularly, and gets plenty of sleep.

6. **Sylvia:** Hello Carol, hello Eugene. Come on in. Make (a) _____ at home. Help (b) _____ to some drinks.

7. **Mother:** Be careful! That pot on the stove is very hot. Don't burn _____.

8. **Cristina:** I know this chocolate is fattening, but it looks so delicious. I can't help _____!

   Billy: Oh, go ahead. One piece is okay!

FOCUS 2	Verbs Commonly Used with Reflexive Pronouns/*By* + Reflexive Pronoun

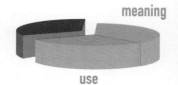

EXAMPLES	EXPLANATIONS
(a) I fell and **hurt myself.** (b) He **taught himself** to play the guitar. (c) Be careful! Don't **cut yourself** with that knife. (d) Did you **enjoy yourself** at the party?	These verbs are commonly used with reflexive pronouns: *hurt* *cut* *tell* *burn* *blame* *enjoy* *teach* *introduce* *behave* *take care of*
(e) He got up, washed, and shaved.	The verbs *wash, dress,* and *shave* do not usually take reflexive pronouns. In sentence (e), it is clear he washed and shaved *himself* and not another person.
(f) He's only 2, but he wants to get dressed **by himself.** (g) I sometimes go to the movies **by myself.**	Use *by* + a reflexive pronoun to show that someone is doing something alone (without help or company).

EXERCISE 3

Write a sentence describing the action in each picture.
Use the verbs in the box.

Examples: *The woman is introducing herself to the man.*
The woman introduced herself to the man.

1.    2.    3.

4.    5.    6.

7.    8.

cut	dry	enjoy	look at/admire
clean/lick	hurt	sing to	weigh

1. _____
2. _____
3. _____
4. _____
5. _____
6. _____
7. _____
8. _____

FOCUS 3 | Reciprocal Pronoun: *Each Other*

The reciprocal pronoun *each other* is different in meaning from a reflexive pronoun.

a. John and Ann blamed **themselves** for the accident.

b. John and Ann blamed **each other** for the accident.

EXERCISE 4

Match the sentence to the picture it describes. Write the letter of the picture next to the sentence.

1. The weather was very hot. The runners poured water on each other after the race.

   The runners poured water on themselves after the race.

2. They love themselves.

   They love each other.

3. The women are fanning themselves because it's so hot.

   The women are fanning each other because it's so hot.

a.

b.

c.

d.

e.

f.

EXERCISE 5

Work with a partner. Act out the following sentences to show the difference between *each other* and reflexive pronouns. Each pair will take turns performing the action in front of the class. The class decides if the action is (a) or (b).

1. a. You and your classmate are looking at yourselves in the mirror.

   b. You and your classmate are looking at each other.

2. a. You and your classmate are talking to yourselves.

   b. You and your classmate are talking to each other.

3. a. You're playing ball with a friend, and you break a neighbor's window. Blame yourself for the accident.

   b. You're playing ball with a friend, and you break a neighbor's window. Blame each other for the accident.

4. a. Introduce yourself to your partner.

   b. You and your partner introduce each other to another person.

5. a. You and your partner are admiring each other.

   b. You and your partner are admiring yourselves.

EXERCISE 6

Choose a reflexive pronoun or *each other* to complete the statements.

1. An egotistical person only thinks about _____himself/herself_____.

2. Divorced people can be friends if they forgive _____.

3. Good friends protect _____.

4. Close friends tell _____ their secrets.

5. A self-confident person believes in _____.

6. In a good relationship, the two people trust _____.

7. A realistic woman doesn't lie to _____.

8. Independent people take care of _____.

9. Caring people help _____.

10. Angry people say things to hurt _____.

11. Young children can't always control _____.

12. An insecure boy doesn't have confidence in _____.

EXERCISE 7

Circle the correct pronoun in the "Dear Darcy" letters below.

Example: (He) / Him / Himself doesn't care about I / (me) / myself.

Dear Darcy,
(1) I / My / Mine boyfriend loves himself. (2) He / His / Him is very pleased with (3) he / him / himself. He always looks at (4) he / him / himself in store windows when he passes by. (5) Himself / He / Him only thinks about (6) his / himself / him. He never brings (7) my / me / myself flowers. The last time he told (8) my / me / myself that he loved me was two years ago. He's also very selfish with (9) he / his / him things. For example, he never lends me (10) him / himself / his car. He says that the car is (11) himself / him / his, and he doesn't want me to use it. Do (12) yourself / your / you have any advice for me?

—Unhappy

Dear Unhappy,

(13) You / Your / Yourself boyfriend certainly is very selfish. (14) You / Your / Yourself can't really change (15) he / himself / him. Get rid of (16) he / himself / him! Do (17) you / yourself / yours a favor. Find (18) you / yourself / yours a new guy!

—Darcy

EXERCISE 8

Correct the errors in the following sentences.

1. I hurt me.

2. They decided to work out the problem theirselves.

3. I shave myself every morning.

4. I have a friend in Poland. We write to ourselves every month.

5. We enjoyed at the circus.

6. After the argument, Alex didn't talk to Sam. Sam didn't talk to Harry. They didn't talk to themselves for a whole year.

7. He did it hisself.

8. Each other said hello.

Use Your English

ACTIVITY 1 writing/speaking

Who is the most independent person in your class?

■ **STEP 1** Work in groups of three. Make up a survey with ten questions to ask your classmates.

Examples: *Do you like to do things by yourself? Do you ever travel by yourself? Do you ever go to the movies by yourself?*

■ **STEP 2** Each student goes to everyone in class and asks the survey questions. Take notes on the responses.

■ **STEP 3** Go back to your group and share the responses. Decide who is the most independent person in class. Compare your results with the results of the other people.

ACTIVITY 2 listening/speaking

CD Track 18

■ **STEP 1** Listen to the Dear Darcy Radio Talk Show callers talk about their problems. Match each problem to the caller.

Caller 1 _____   a. Frantic about Finances

Caller 2 _____   b. Ms. No Confidence

Caller 3 _____   c. Lonely Without Love

■ **STEP 2** Imagine you are the radio talk show host. What advice can you give to each of these people? Tell your classmates.

ACTIVITY 3 writing

■ **STEP 1** Write a letter to Dear Darcy about a problem you have. Choose a problem you are comfortable sharing with your partner.

■ **STEP 2** Work with a partner. Exchange your letters and write a response to the problem.

ACTIVITY 4 speaking

■ **STEP 1** Talk about a good relationship you have with another person—friend or family. Describe what you do for each other, how you support each other, how you help each other, and how you feel about each other.

■ **STEP 2** Talk about two nations or two groups within a nation and describe a political, economic, or social problem such as what they did to each other, how they hurt each other, and if they worked out a solution to their problems.

ACTIVITY 5 research on the web

 Search the Internet for *advice* on *student English language learning*. Enter those keywords into a search engine such as Google®, Yahoo®, or Ask®. Choose one page of advice, print it out, and bring it to class. Make a list of good advice on English language learning. Do you and your classmates agree or disagree with the advice?

ACTIVITY 6 reflection

How do you see yourself as a language learner? Write a paragraph using the topic sentence: *"I see myself as a successful/unsuccessful language learner."* Use your sentence responses to the questions to support your topic sentence.

YOUR EMOTIONS	YOUR LEARNING STRATEGIES
1. Do you feel confident in yourself as a language learner?	7. Do you set goals for yourself?
2. Do you ever compare yourself to other students in the class?	8. Do you repeat new words to yourself?
3. Do you tell yourself you can do it?	9. Do you ask yourself questions about a reading or listening text?
4. Are you proud of yourself? Disappointed in yourself?	10. Do you correct yourself?
5. Do you push yourself to learn more?	11. Do you try to solve language problems by yourself?
6. Do you get angry at yourself about errors?	12. Do you listen to yourself on tape?

FUTURE TIME
Will and *Be Going To, May* and *Might*

- Talk about future time using *will, be going to, may,* and *might*

- Understand the meaning and position of future time expressions

- Choose between *will* and *be going to* when
  - talking about future intentions or plans
  - making predictions

OPENING TASK
Are You an Optimist or a Pessimist?

Do you see this glass as half full or half empty?

If you see it as half full, you are a positive person, or an optimist.

If you see it as half empty, you are a negative person, or a pessimist.

■ STEP 1

Work with a partner. Write statements about the future using the information below. Your statements can be affirmative or negative.

Within the next twenty-five years, . . .

1. Wars / end

   _____

2. People everywhere / have enough food to eat

   _____

3. Governments / take care of their people's needs

   _____

4. People in all countries / have a good life

   _____

5. Men and women around the world / be equal

   _____

6. People / take care of the earth

   _____

7. All the world's children / learn to read and write

   _____

8. People / live on the moon

   _____

9. Scientists / find a cure for AIDS

   _____

10. The world / speak one universal language

   _____

■ STEP 2

Look at your answers. Are you an optimist or a pessimist? (Note: more than five negative responses indicate that you are a pessimist!) Share your answers with the class.

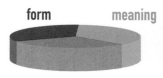
FOCUS 1   Talking About Future Time

Use *will* and *be going to* to make predictions about the future or to say what you think will happen in the future.

EXAMPLES	EXPLANATIONS
(a) One day, he **will** be rich.	Use *will* for a prediction (what we think will happen).
(b) Look at those big black clouds. It **is going to** rain.	Use *be going to* for a prediction based on the present situation (what we can see is going to happen).
(c) NOT: It will rain.	
(d) Teacher to student: Your parents **will** be very upset about this.	*Will* is more formal.
(e) Father to daughter: Your mother's **going to** be very angry about this.	*Be going to* is less formal.

EXERCISE 1

Match the sentences on the next page to these pictures.

a.

b.

c.

d.

e.

f.

g.

1. _____ Look at that waiter! He's going to fall!

2. _____ This marriage isn't going to last.

3. _____ You will find gold on the streets of America!

4. _____ She's going to get a headache.

5. _____ I will always love you.

6. _____ You will grow up and be famous.

7. _____ Be careful, Julian. You're going to fall!

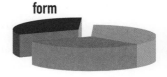

form

FOCUS 2 · *Will*

AFFIRMATIVE STATEMENTS		NEGATIVE STATEMENTS	
I He She It We You They	**will arrive** next week. **'ll arrive** next week.	I He She It We You They	**will not arrive** next week. **won't arrive** next week.
There	**will be** peace in the world. **'ll be** peace in the world.	There	**will not be** any wars. **won't be** any wars.
Men	**will be able to** stay home with their children. **'ll be able to** stay home with their children.	Men	**will not be able to** have children. **won't be able to** have children.

YES/NO QUESTIONS			SHORT ANSWERS					
			Affirmative			Negative		
Will	I you he she it we you they	arrive next week?	Yes,	you I he she it you we they	**will.**	No,	you I he she it you we they	**won't.**

WH-QUESTIONS	ANSWERS
(a) **Who will** get an Olympic medal?	The snowboarder.
(b) **What will** the homeless woman do with the money?	She'll **change her life**.
(c) **When will** scientists discover a cure for AIDS?	(They **will discover** a cure)* within six years.
(d) **Where will** the couple retire?	(They **will retire**) to Hawaii.
(e) **How will** the couple travel to Hawaii?	(They'll **travel**) by plane.
(f) **How** long **will** they be on the plane?	(They'll **be** on the plane) for five hours.
(g) **Why** will this doctor be successful?	because she cares about her patients.
(h) **Who(m) will** the doctor save?	(She'll **save**) many patients.

* Note: The parentheses (...) show the part of the answer that is often not said in spoken English.

EXERCISE 2

How will our lives be different in fifty years? Make predictions with *will* or *won't*. Discuss your predictions with a partner.

1. Cities _____ be very crowded.

2. Many people _____ eat only fruits and vegetables.

3. All countries _____ share the world's money equally.

4. Most people _____ move back to the countryside.

5. Cell phones _____ be the size of our thumb.

6. Most people _____ go to college.

7. All people of different races _____ live together peacefully.

8. Robots _____ take over some human jobs.

9. Crime _____ go down.

10. People _____ drive electric cars.

11. Students _____ take classes from home by satellite.

12. Science _____ continue to be very important.

13. Most people _____ work sixty hours a week.

14. A woman _____ be president of the United States.

EXERCISE 3

Think about the year 2025. Write *yes/no* questions with *will*. Interview two classmates and report their answers to the class.

	Classmate 1	Classmate 2
1. be in the United States *Will you be in the United States?* _____	_____	_____
2. speak English fluently _____	_____	_____
3. be back in your home country _____	_____	_____
4. have a good job _____	_____	_____
5. have children _____	_____	_____
6. live in the city or country _____	_____	_____
7. be happy _____	_____	_____
8. want something different _____	_____	_____
9. write to your friends from our ESL class _____	_____	_____

Add two questions of your own.

10. _____	_____	_____
11. _____	_____	_____

EXERCISE 4

How will life be different in a hundred years? Work in a group of four. Take turns asking and answering *yes/no* questions with *will*. Discuss your predictions with the group.

Example: 1. *Will the climate change?*
   a. The Environment
1. the climate / change
2. hurricanes and earthquakes / get stronger
3. pollution / get worse

b. The Family

1. The traditional family with a husband, wife, and two children / disappear

2. Men and women / continue to marry

3. Girls / have the same opportunities as boys

c. Science and Health

1. We / discover life on other planets

2. People / vacation on the moon

3. People / live to be 150 years old

EXERCISE 5

Work in groups of three. Make one question about the future with *there + be* in Column A. Make *yes/no* questions with *be able to* in Column B. Discuss your answers to these questions.

Example: 1.   a.   *Will there be wars?*
                     b.   Will the UN be able to stop wars? Will soldiers be able to say "no" to war?

COLUMN A: THERE + BE	COLUMN B: BE ABLE TO
1. wars	1. a. The United Nations / stop wars
	b. Soldiers / say "no" to war
2. new sources of energy	2. a. We / heat our homes
	b. We / drive our cars
3. good governments	3. a. People / vote
	b. People / speak freely
4. economic equality	4. a. The poor / feed their children
	b. The poor / get health care
5. new medicines	5. a. Doctors / cure cancer
	b. Doctors / treat new diseases like bird flu

Wally the Worry Wart Meets Fanny the Fortune Teller

Wally the Worry Wart

Fanny the Fortune Teller

Work with a partner. You are Wally the Worry Wart. Your partner is Fanny the Fortune Teller. Ask your partner *yes/no* and *wh-questions* with *will*. Your partner will create a possible story for Mr. Worry Wart. Compare your stories with those of your classmates. Decide if your fortune teller partner is an optimist or a pessimist!

Example: You: *Will I go to college?*
  Your partner: *Yes, you will. / No, you won't.*

Mr. Worry Wart's Questions

1. I / go to college
2. How / I / pay for college
3. I / graduate from college
4. What / I do after college
5. Who / give me a job
6. I / earn a good salary
7. Whom / I marry
8. Where / we live
9. We / be able to / have children
10. Our children / be healthy
11. My wife and I / be able to / retire
12. Who / take care of us
13. How many grandchildren / we have
14. How long / we live
15. I / be a worry wart forever

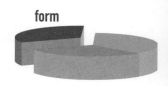

form

FOCUS 3   *Be Going To*

AFFIRMATIVE STATEMENTS		
I	am 'm	
He She It	is 's	going to leave.
We You They	are 're	

NEGATIVE STATEMENTS		
I	am not 'm not	
He She It	is not isn't	going to leave.
We You They	are not aren't	

YES/NO QUESTIONS			SHORT ANSWERS						
Am	I				you	are.		you	aren't.
Are	you	going to leave?	Yes,	I	am.	No,	I	'm not.
Is	he she it			he she it	is.		he she it	isn't.
Are	we you they			we you they	are.		we you they	aren't.

WH-QUESTIONS			ANSWERS	
When		leave?		leave in two weeks.
Where		go?		go to Colorado.
What		do there?		go skiing.
How	are you going to	get there?	I'm going to	go by car.
How long		stay?		stay for one week.
Who(m)		visit?		visit my cousin.
Who's	going to	drive?	My friend	(is going to drive).

NOTE: *Going to* is often pronounced "gonna" when we speak. We do not usually write "gonna."

Look at the pictures. Then fill in the blanks with the affirmative or negative form of *be going to*.

1.  "Watch out! That bag _____ fall!"

2.  "Hurry up! We _____ miss the bus."

3.  "This _____ hurt you one bit."

4.  "I am so tired! I _____ take a nap."

5.  "Hello, dear. I _____ be home on time tonight."

6.

George: What are you _____ have, Fred?

Fred: I _____ have a pizza, as usual.

7.

"Watch her, Jack! She _____ fall into the pool!"

8.

"They _____ have a baby today."

9.

"Hello, boss. I'm sorry, I _____ be able to come in today. I have a terrible backache, and I can't get out of bed."

10.

Ben: I have a test tomorrow. I _____ study.

Roommate: I have a test tomorrow too, but I _____ study. I _____ watch the game on TV!

EXERCISE 8

This is a conversation between Wally and Robert. Read the answers. Write a yes/no question or wh-question with *be going to*. The first one has been done for you.

Wally: My doctor says I have too much stress. I need to leave my job and get away somewhere.

Robert: (1) _____ Where are you going to go _____?

Wally: To California.

Robert: (2) _____?
Wally: I don't know (what I'm going to do there).
Robert: (3) _____?
Wally: (I'm going to stay) with some old friends.
Robert: (4) _____?
Wally: For about a month.
Robert: (5) _____?
Wally: By plane.
Robert: (6) _____?
Wally: I don't know (if I'm going to come back to my job).

EXERCISE 9

STEP 1   Match the phrases to the correct person/people.
Then, make a statement about each person's future, using *be going to*.

_____ 1. A bald man	a. inherit one million dollars from an uncle
_____ 2. An athlete	b. win an Olympic gold medal
_____ 3. A teenager	c. have ten grandchildren
_____ 4. A movie director	d. open his own restaurant
_____ 5. A lifeguard	e. write best-selling books
_____ 6. A chef	f. produce a new movie and win an Oscar
_____ 7. A homeless man	g. find a cure for the common cold
_____ 8. A scientist	h. save someone's life
_____ 9. An elderly couple	i. grow hair on his head
_____ 10. An author	j. graduate and become a famous rock star

STEP 2   Make one optimistic and one pessimistic prediction using *be going to* for each person.

Example: *The bald man is going to marry a beautiful woman.* (optimistic prediction)
The bald man is going to color his hair green. (pessimistic prediction)

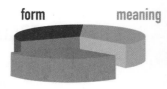

FOCUS 4   Time Expressions in the Future

EXAMPLES	EXPLANATIONS
(a) I'm going to visit you **tomorrow evening**. (b) **A month from now,** Fanny will be on a tropical island.	Future time expressions can come at the beginning or at the end of the sentence. Put a comma (,) after the time expression when it is at the beginning of the sentence.

Future Time Expressions

(later) this	morning afternoon evening	next	week month year Sunday weekend	tomorrow	morning afternoon evening night	soon later the day after tomorrow a week from today tonight

EXAMPLES	EXPLANATIONS
I'll see you	We also use prepositional phrases of time to talk about future time.

(c) **in**   fifteen minutes.
       two weeks.
       March.
       2015.
	Use *in* with part of a day or a longer period.

(d) **on** Tuesday. May 21st.	Use *on* with a specific day.
(e) **at** 4:00. midnight.	Use *at* with clock time.
(f) We are going to go to the Bahamas **for** three weeks.	*For* shows how long the action will last.
(g) I'll be there **until** 3:00. (At 3:00, I will leave. I will not be there after 3:00.) (h) I won't be there **until** Monday. (Before Monday, I won't be there. After Monday, I'll be there.)	*Until* shows the specific time in the future when the action will change.

EXERCISE 10

Look at Fanny's calendar. Imagine it is now 2:00 P.M. on Wednesday, April 10. Read the sentences about Fanny's plans, and fill in the blanks with a time expression or a preposition of time. There may be more than one correct answer.

APRIL

SUNDAY	MONDAY	TUESDAY	WEDNESDAY	THURSDAY	FRIDAY	SATURDAY
0	1	2	3	4	5	6
7	8	9	10 Last client 6:00 pm	11 polish crystal ball	12 deposit money in bank	13
14	15	16 buy new fortune cards	17	18 secretary goes on vacation	19 Fortune Tellers' conference	20
21	22	23	24	25	26	
28	29	30				

STILL TO DO:
First Edition of "How to Make Predictions" magazine arrives on June 10th
Retire 2015!
Write my autobiography 2020

MAY

SUNDAY	MONDAY	TUESDAY	WEDNESDAY	THURSDAY	FRI	AY
			1	2	3	4
5	6 place ad in newspaper	7	8	9	10	11
12	13	14	15			

1. Fanny is going to see her last client _at 6:00 this evening/in four hours_.
2. She's going to attend the Fortune Tellers' Conference _____.
3. She's going to polish her crystal ball _____.
4. She's going to deposit all her money in the bank _____.
5. Her secretary is going to go on vacation _____.
6. She is going to buy new fortune cards _____.
7. She's going to put an advertisement about herself in the newspaper
   _____.
8. She will read her first *How To Make Predictions* magazine _____.
9. She will retire to a tropical island _____.
10. She will write a book called *How to Be a Successful Fortune Teller in 10 Easy Lessons*
    _____.

EXERCISE 11

Make statements about yourself. Use *be going to*.

Example: In a few days, <u>I'm going to move out of my apartment.</u>

1. In a few days, ————————————————————————.
2. Next summer, ————————————————————————.
3. The day after tomorrow, ————————————————————.
4. This evening, ————————————————————————.
5. Tomorrow night, ————————————————————————.
6. This weekend, ————————————————————————.
7. At 9:00 P.M., ————————————————————————.
8. In December, ————————————————————————.
9. On Wednesday night, ————————————————————————.
10. On New Year's Eve, ————————————————————————.

FOCUS 5	Talking About Future Intentions or Plans

use

EXAMPLES	EXPLANATIONS
(a) **A:** The phone is ringing. **B:** O.K. I'll get it.	Use *will* when you decide to do something **at** the time of speaking.
(b) **Mother:** Where are you going? **Daughter:** I'm going to take a drive with Richard tonight. Remember, Mom? You said it was okay . . . **Mother:** I did?	Use *be going to* when you made a plan to do something **before** the time of speaking.

Work with a partner. You read the first five statements in Column A aloud. Your partner chooses an answer from Column B. After the first five, your partner reads from Column A and you choose the answer from Column B.

Example: Do you have any plans for tonight?   a. Yes, we will go to the theater.

b. Yes, we're going to the theater.

Column A	Column B
1. Christine called. She's coming over for dinner.	a. Great! I'll cook. b. Great! I'm going to cook.
2. What are you doing with that camera?	a. I'll take your picture. b. I'm going to take your picture.
3. Do you need a ride home today?	a. No, thanks. Andrew will take me home. b. No, thanks. Andrew's going to take me home.
4. We don't have a thing to eat in the house.	a. I'll call up and order a pizza. b. I'm going to call up and order a pizza.
5. Help! The car died again.	a. Calm down. I'll be right there. b. Calm down. I'm going to be right there.
6. Why are you meeting Jenny in the library tonight?	a. She'll help me with my homework. b. She's going to help me with my homework.
7. Look, those thieves are robbing the bank!	a. I'll call the police. b. I'm going to call the police.
8. Mom, can you brush my hair?	a. I'll do it in a minute, sweetie. b. I'm going to do it in a minute, sweetie.
9. Are you off the phone yet?	a. I'll be off in a minute! b. I'm going to be off in a minute!
10. Why did Maria cancel her date for Saturday night?	a. Her parents will take her away for the weekend. b. Her parents are going to take her away for the weekend.

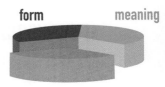

form   meaning

FOCUS 6   *May* and *Might*

Use *may* or *might* to say something is possible in the future

EXAMPLES	EXPLANATIONS
(a) I **will go** to Mexico next year.	(a) shows certainty The speaker is 100 percent sure.
(b) I **may/might go** to Mexico next year.	(b) shows possibility The speaker is 50 percent sure.

AFFIRMATIVE STATEMENTS			NEGATIVE STATEMENTS		
I He She We You They	**may** **might**	study abroad next year. be able to stay abroad.	I He She We You They	**may not** **might not**	take a vacation. be able to stay for two years.
It		rain later.	It		rain later.
There		be cheap flights to Mexico.	There		be any discounts on flights.

NOTE: There are no contractions for *may* or *might*.

EXERCISE 13

What's it like to be Wally the Worry Wart? Fill in the blanks with *may* or *might* in the affirmative or negative.

1. Wally on the Weather

   Wally: Look at those clouds! It'll definitely rain today.

   Wife: No, Wally. It (a) _____ clear up and be a beautiful day. I think we (b) _____ be able to have a picnic this afternoon.

   Wally: But the grass (c) _____ be wet; and we (d) _____ be able to sit down.

   Wife: Relax, the sun will dry it out, Wally!

2. Wally on Vacation

   Friend: Are you going to try skiing, Wally?

   Wally: I (a) _____. On second thought, the slopes (b) _____ be icy, and I (c) _____ fall and break my neck! I think I'll stay in the lodge and drink hot chocolate!

   Friend: You (d) _____ miss a great experience. . . .

   Wally: But I won't break any bones!

3. Wally on the Traffic from his Cell Phone:

   Wally: Hello, honey. I (a) _____ be home in time for dinner tonight. The traffic is awful. I'm afraid I (b) _____ have an accident. I (c) _____ have enough gas to get home! You (d) _____ need to come get me.

4. Wally on His New Job

   Wally: I (a) _____ last long at this new job, honey.

   Wife: Why not?

   Wally: Well, I (b) _____ like it. And my boss (c) _____ like me. The salary (d) _____ be too good.

   Wife: You'll be fine. Don't worry so much, Wally.

EXERCISE 14

STEP 1 What are your plans for the future? Interview your partner and answer your partner's questions. Complete the chart with your partner's information. Then report your partner's plans to the class.

Example: **You:** *What are you going to do this evening?*
Your partner: *I'm going to see a movie this weekend.*

	BASE VERB	WILL/BE GOING TO	MAY/MIGHT
1. this evening	see a movie	✔	
2. this weekend	study at home		✔
3. tomorrow night			
4. a week from today			
5. in three months			
6. next summer			
7. in five years			

STEP 2 Use the information from Step 1 to write statements about your partner's definite or possible plans.

EXERCISE 15

Look into your crystal ball again. What is our future ten years from now? Make statements with affirmative or negative forms of *will, be going to, may,* or *might.*

Example: Europe / be a superpower
In ten years, Europe will be a superpower.

1. People / want to go back to the simple days before computers
2. People around the world /move away from big cities
3. China and India / become superpowers
4. Solar energy / be the most common source of energy
5. Students in classrooms all around the world / be able to see and talk to each other
6. Books / disappear completely
7. There / be cures for cancer, bird flu, and other fatal diseases
8. The planet Earth / be 10 degrees warmer

Use Your English

ACTIVITY **1** writing/speaking

What do you think the world will be like in 2050? Think about changes in the environment, the family, in science, health, and technology. With your group, write down ten changes. Discuss your group's ideas with the rest of the class.

ACTIVITY **2** speaking

Role-play the Optimist and the Pessimist. Work with a partner. Make pessimistic statements about your future OR the future of the world. Your partner tries to make you feel better by making more optimistic statements about you / the world.

Example: You: *I will never learn English!*

Your partner: *It may take you a little longer, but you will learn!*

ACTIVITY 3 listening

CD Track 19

Every year, Americans make New Year's Resolutions. They promise to do something to change their lives in the future. Listen to three people from this unit talk about their New Year's resolutions. Identify the person who is speaking. Choose from the people in the box.

Wally the Worry Wart	A chef	Fanny the Fortune Teller
A doctor	A homeless man	A teenage rock star

Person 1: _____

Person 2: _____

Person 3: _____

ACTIVITY 4 writing

■ **STEP 1**   Sit in a circle with your whole class or a group of six to eight people. On the top of a blank piece of paper, write:

On _____ in the year 2020, _____
　　　　(today's date)　　　　　　　　　　　　(your name)

■ **STEP 2**   Pass the sheet of paper to the person on your left. This person writes a prediction about you for the year 2020. Then he or she passes the paper to the left for the next person to write a second prediction.

■ **STEP 3**   Continue until everyone has written their predictions. At the end of the activity, you will have a list of predictions. Read the predictions and choose the best one. Read it aloud to the class.

ACTIVITY 5 research on the web

 Search the Internet for the weather forecast for a city you want to visit next week. Use a search engine such as Google®, Ask®, or Yahoo® and enter the keyword: *weather* and the name of your city or town. Share the seven day or next week's weather prediction for your city with a partner. Tell your partner about any special items you will bring for your trip.

Example: *Next week, it will rain in Seattle. It's going to be 60 degrees. I'm going to bring my umbrella and raincoat.*

ACTIVITY 6 reflection

■ **STEP 1** Make yourself a Learning Plan using the table below. Write a list of goals, and decide when you will reach each goal (next week, in two months, next year, in June…). Discuss your Learning Plan with a partner.

My Learning Plan

MY GOALS	WHEN I WILL ACCOMPLISH MY GOALS
1. I will learn fifty new vocabulary words.	in four months
2.	
3.	
4.	
5.	
6.	
7.	

■ **STEP 2** Write an entry in your Learning Journal about your goals and when you will accomplish them.

PHRASAL VERBS

UNIT GOALS

- Understand the meaning of common phrasal verbs

- Know which phrasal verbs are separable and inseparable phrasal verbs

- Learn which phrasal verbs take objects and which do not take objects

OPENING TASK
What's a Technophobe To Do?

▪ STEP 1

A *technophobe* is someone who is afraid of/not good with technology. Create a questionnaire to identify the technophobes in your class. Complete each question with a word from the box. You may use a word more than once.

out	up	call
give	take	back
away	wake	break
turn	on	

Questionnaire

When your computer doesn't work,

1. Do you bring it _____ to the store?

2. Do you throw it _____ and buy a new computer?

3. Do you back _____ all your files?

4. Do you _____ up a computer specialist?

5. Do you _____ out the computer manual and read it?

6. Do you try to figure _____ what to do by yourself?

7. Do you _____ off the computer?

8. Do you turn it _____ again?

9. Do you _____ up and do your work by hand?

10. Do you _____ down and cry?

■ STEP 2

Who are the technophobes in your class? Give your reasons.

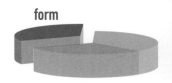

form

FOCUS 1   Phrasal Verbs

EXAMPLES	EXPLANATION
(a) **Turn on** the lights. (b) **Take out** the garbage.	Phrasal verbs are special verbs that have two parts: a verb + a particle. The combination of the verb and particle creates a new meaning. *turn + on* *take + out*

EXERCISE 1

Go back to your questionnaire in the Opening Task on page 345. List all the phrasal verbs.

FOCUS 2   Phrasal Verbs

meaning

use

EXAMPLES	EXPLANATIONS
(a) Plants **grow**. (*grow* = to increase in size) (b) Children **grow up**. (*grow up* = to become an adult)	The verb + particle have a specific meaning. This new meaning can be different from the meaning of the verb or the meaning of the particle.
(c) The speaker **sat down**.	Sometimes the meaning of a phrasal verb is clear from the verb + particle.
(d) I **ran into** Joe on the street the other day. It was great to see him again after so many years.	Sometimes it is difficult to guess the meaning of a phrasal verb. Sometimes the context of the sentence can help you. The meaning of *run into* is not the combination of *run* and *into*. *Run into* means "to meet someone by chance."
(e) I **filled out** the college application. (f) Richie **filled up** the tank with gas.	The same verb can have a different meaning with a different particle. *fill + out* = to complete *fill + up* = to fill
(g) Please **put out** your cigarette, Jake. (h) Please **extinguish** your cigarettes, ladies and gentlemen.	In informal English, phrasal verbs are more frequent than one-word verbs with the same meaning. In (g), you are talking to a friend. In (h), an announcer is speaking to passengers at a train station.

EXERCISE 2

Read each statement on the left to your partner. Your partner chooses a response from the right.

Statement

1. I don't want to cook tonight.
2. It's hot in here.
3. It's so quiet in here.
4. I can't read the map. The print is too small.
5. I can't do my homework with the TV on.
6. I'm bored.
7. My feet hurt.
8. I'm sleepy.
9. I'm really upset about our argument today.
10. I'm tired of sitting on this plane.

Response

a. Let's calm down and talk about it.
b. Call up a friend.
c. Stand up and walk around for a few minutes.
d. Sit down for a while.
e. Lie down and take a nap.
f. Take off your jacket.
g. Put on your glasses.
h. Turn off the TV.
i. Let's eat out.
j. Turn on the radio.

EXERCISE 3

Work with a partner. Underline the phrasal verbs in the sentences below. Then try to guess the meaning of each phrasal verb in the context of the sentence.

1. A procrastinator puts off chores until tomorrow.
2. A healthy eater doesn't fill up on sweets.
3. A clown cheers up his audience.
4. A saver never throws away anything.
5. A good reader doesn't look up every word in the dictionary.
6. A quitter never sees through any of his projects.
7. A champion never gives up.
8. A neat person always hangs up his clothes.

Circle the phrasal verbs. Then match each phrasal verb with a one-word verb.

Sentences with phrasal verbs

One-word verb with same meaning

1. I called 911 Emergency. The firefighters will be here soon to (put out) the fire. __d__

2. Don't just stand at the door. Come in. _____

3. Fill out the application. _____

4. We're going to practice some phrasal verbs. Henry, can you please hand out this exercise? _____

5. I left my book at school. I don't remember the homework for tonight. I'll call up Manny and ask him. _____

6. I can't talk to you now. Please come back in fifteen minutes. _____

7. I can't concentrate! Would you please turn down the music! _____

8. I am freezing in this house. Please turn up the heat. _____

9. Please take off your wet shoes. _____

10. Hold on a minute. I'm not ready yet. _____

a. raise

b. remove

c. telephone

d. extinguish

e. enter

f. distribute

g. complete

h. wait

i. lower

j. return

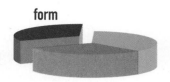

form

FOCUS 3 — Separable Phrasal Verbs

EXAMPLES	EXPLANATIONS
	Many phrasal verbs take direct objects. When the direct object is a **noun**, it can go:

	Verb	Particle	D.O.	
(a) The teacher	handed	out	the exercise.	after the particle

	Verb	D.O.	Particle	
(b) The teacher	**handed**	the exercise	**out.**	between the verb and the particle

(c) The teacher handed **it** out.

(d) NOT: The teacher handed out **it**.

When the direct object is a **pronoun**, it always goes between the verb and the particle.

Common Separable Phrasal Verbs

SEPARABLE PHRASAL VERBS	EXAMPLES	MEANING
calm down	(a) She is very upset about the accident. We can't **calm** her **down.**	Become quiet or calm
call up	(b) I **called** my friend **up** the other night to ask about the homework.	telephone
cheer up	(c) My friend failed her final exam, so I brought her flowers to **cheer** her **up.**	become happy, make someone happy
clean up	(d) Your room's a mess. **Clean** it **up**!	clean
figure out	(e) This puzzle is very confusing. I can't **figure** it **out.**	solve, understand
fill out	(f) Here's an application. **Fill** it **out** for a new license.	complete
fill up	(g) **Fill** it **up** with regular gas, please.	fill

Continued on next page

SEPARABLE PHRASAL VERBS	EXAMPLES	MEANING
hand out	(h) The teacher **handed** the tests **out** to the class.	distribute
hang up	(i) My husband never **hangs** his clothes **up**. (j) Please **hang up** the phone.	place on a hanger or a hook
look up	(k) I didn't know his telephone number, so I **looked** it **up** in the phone book.	search for in a reference book
pick up	(l) In my neighborhood, they **pick** the garbage **up** every Tuesday. (m) What time do you **pick** your children **up** from school?	collect, lift
put away	(n) My kids are neat! They always **put** their toys **away**.	put in its usual place
put off	(o) Do it now. Don't **put** it **off** until tomorrow.	postpone
put on	(p) It's really cold outside, so **put** your coat **on**.	dress yourself
put out	(q) It took firefighters a few hours to **put** the fire **out**.	extinguish
take off	(r) **Take** your shoes **off** before you come into the house.	remove
take out	(s) Will you please **take** the garbage **out**?	put something outside
throw out/away	(t) I have a lot of old things in the garage. I need to **throw** them **out**.	dispose of, put in garbage
turn down	(u) It's 2:00 in the morning. **Turn** that stereo **down**!	lower the volume
turn off	(v) There aren't any good programs on TV tonight. **Turn** it **off**.	stop the power
turn on	(w) I always **turn** the radio **on** in the morning.	start the power
turn up	(x) When I hear my favorite song, I **turn** the volume **up**.	increase the volume
wake up	(y) It's 7:00. Time to **wake up**! (z) The baby's sleeping. Don't **wake** him **up**.	to become awake

Sergeant Strict is giving orders to his new soldiers. He's losing his patience and getting very frustrated. Repeat the Sergeant's orders in a different way each time.

1. a. "Take off your civilian clothes."

   b. "I said, _____ take your civilian clothes off _____."

   c. "Come on, _____ take them off _____!"

2. a. "Hand out these uniforms."

   b. "I said, _____."

   c. "Come on, _____!"

3. a. "Put on your new Army clothes."

   b. "I said, _____."

   c. "Come on, _____!"

4. a. "Turn down that radio."

   b. "I said, _____."

   c. "Come on, _____!"

5. a. "Put away your old clothes."

   b. "I said, _____."

   c. "Come on, _____!"

6. a. "Throw out that junk food from home."

   b. "I said, _____."

   c. "Come on, _____!"

7. a. "Clean up this mess."

   b. "I said, _____."

   c. "Come on, _____!"

8. a. "Turn off the lights!"

   b. "I said, _____."

   c. "Come on, _____!"

EXERCISE 6

Fill in the blanks with the phrasal verbs below. Use a pronoun in the second blank of each dialogue.

Example: (clean up)

Mother: Danny, don't forget to (a) _____clean up_____ the mess in your bedroom.

Danny: Mom, I (b) _____cleaned it up_____ this morning.

figure out	pick up	cheer up	hand out	throw out	fill out

1. **Counselor:** You need to (a) _____ this application for college.

   Abdul: Can I (b) _____ at home?

2. **Susie:** Danny, I think it's time to (a) _____ all these old newspapers.

   Danny: I'm (b) _____ right now.

3. **Jackie:** Could you please (a) _____ that paper on the floor for me?

   Mark: I'll (b) _____ in a minute!

4. **Ms. Wagner:** Can you help me (a) _____ these exams, John?

   John: Sure, I'll (b) _____ right now.

5. **Mom:** Please try to (a) _____ your sister. She's in a bad mood!

   Bobbie: No one can (b) _____. She's always in a bad mood.

6. **Liz:** Can you (a) _____ the directions for this software program, Felicia?

   Felicia: I can't, but I'm sure that Sayeed could (b) _____.

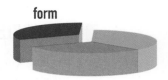

FOCUS 4 | Inseparable Phrasal Verbs

EXAMPLES	EXPLANATIONS
(a) I **ran into** an old friend on the street. (b) I **ran into** her on the street. (c) NOT: I **ran** an old friend **into** on the street. (d) NOT: I **ran** her **into** on the street.	Some phrasal verbs are inseparable. The direct object—noun or pronoun—always goes after the particle.

Common Inseparable Phrasal Verbs

INSEPARABLE PHRASAL VERBS	EXAMPLES	MEANING
get in *get out of*	(a) I **got in** my car and drove away. (b) I dropped my bag when I **got out of** the cab.	enter and leave a vehicle (car, taxi, truck)
get on *get off*	(c) I **got on** the train at 42nd Street. (d) I **got off** the bus in front of the school.	enter and leave other forms of transportation (bus, plane, train)
go over	(e) How many times did you **go over** your notes before the test? (f) I **went over** them three times before the test. I **went over** them all morning.	review
run into	(g) I **ran into** an old friend the other day.	meet by chance

Fill in the blanks with the correct inseparable phrasal verb. Refer to Focus 4 on page 353 if necessary.

Mandy: It's strange that we live in the same neighborhood, but we never (1) _____ _____ each other.

Sharon: Our schedules are so different.

Mandy: I know! When you (2) _____ _____ _____ work, I go in. When I (3) _____ _____ the bus, you (4) _____ _____.

Sharon: We need to make a date. (5) _____ _____ your calendar and give me a call.

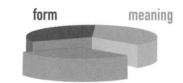

form   meaning

FOCUS 5   Phrasal Verbs Without Objects

Some phrasal verbs do not take an object. These phrasal verbs are inseparable.

PHRASAL VERBS	EXAMPLES	MEANING
break down	(a) My car **broke down** last night, so I walked home.	stop working
come back	(b) He left home and never **came back**.	return
come in	(c) **Come in** and make yourself comfortable.	enter
eat out	(d) I hate to cook, so I often **eat out**.	eat in a restaurant
grow up	(e) I **grew up** in the United States.	become an adult
show up	(f) After two hours, he finally **showed up**.	appear
sit down	(g) I feel tired, so I think I'll **sit down** for a while.	sit
stand up	(h) In some countries, students **stand up** to show respect when the teacher enters the room.	stand

Fill in the blanks with a phrasal verb from the box.

stand up	sit down	break down	eat out
show up	come in	come back	grow up

What do you say when . . .

1. you are very late for an important date?
   You say: "Oh, I'm so sorry. Please forgive me, my car _____."

2. your friend's dog runs away from home?
   You say: "Don't worry, Elliot; I'm sure she'll _____ home very soon."

3. your child is sitting and an elderly man is standing on the bus?
   You say: "_____ and give that man your seat."

4. your 30-year-old friend is acting like a child?
   You say: "Come on, Matt, _____. You're not a child anymore."

5. you are a car salesperson and you are trying to get people into your showroom?
   You say: "Please _____, folks. We have many new models and great prices this year."

6. you and your roommate are hungry, but you're too tired to cook?
   You say: "Let's _____."

7. your friend Cheryl is crying about her date last night?
   You say: "What happened, Cheryl? Don't tell me your date didn't _____ last night."
   Cheryl: "Oh, he did! That's why I'm crying!"

8. you are a receptionist in a very busy doctor's office and an angry patient is complaining about waiting so long?
   You say: "Please _____, Mr. Brody. The doctor will be with you in a few minutes."

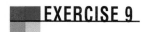

STEP 1   Make a story by putting the pictures in the correct order. Write the number for the order of each picture next to the letter.

a. _____

b. _____

c. _____

d. _____

fill up	look up	break down
figure out	wake up	calm down
turn on	get out of	take out

It was a cold and lonely night. Forgetful Phil was on his way to visit his mother when his car suddenly (1) _____. He was angry and upset, but after a while, he (2) _____. It was dark, so Phil (3) _____ a flashlight from the glove compartment. Then he took out his car manual. He tried to (4) _____, *"What to do when your car breaks down in the middle of nowhere,"* but he didn't find anything in the manual. Next, he (5) _____ the car and looked under the hood. He wasn't able to (6) _____ what the problem was. Then Phil began to understand. He asked himself, "Did I (7) _____ my tank with gas?" The answer, of course, was no.

Luckily there was a house nearby. He knocked on the door and shouted, but nobody answered. There were no other houses. There was no telephone. "What now?" thought Phil. Then, just as he turned around to go back to his car, another car crashed into the back of his car. Suddenly, the people in the house (8) _____ and (9) _____ the lights. Poor Phil felt like crying.

Use Your English

ACTIVITY 1 writing/speaking

Work with a partner. Write a story or dialogue about the situation below, using the phrasal verbs in the box. You may use other phrasal verbs if you want to. Then role-play the situation for the class.

Situation: It is 11:00 P.M. You are sleeping very deeply. Suddenly, you hear some noise coming from the apartment downstairs. Your neighbor's stereo is very loud.

wake up	throw out	turn down	turn off
turn on	go back	calm down	call up

ACTIVITY 2 speaking

Work in a group or as a whole class. The first person begins a story. He or she says, "I woke up . . ." and completes the sentence. The second person repeats the first sentence and adds a second sentence using a phrasal verb. The third person repeats the first two sentences and then adds a third, and so on. Try not to write anything down. Use your memory! Refer to the phrasal verbs in this unit.

Examples: **Player 1:** *I woke up early.*

Player 2: *I woke up early, and turned off the alarm clock.*

Player 3: *I woke up early, turned off the alarm clock, and took off my pajamas.*

■ **STEP 1** Work in a group. Put numbers 1 to 12 in a bag. Pick a number from the bag. Read the sentence in the box that corresponds to your number and then do the action.

■ **STEP 2** After the group has done all the actions, write sentences about the things you did.

Examples: *Mario put on Marcela's cap.*
José turned off the light.

1. Put on a piece of a classmate's clothing or jewelry.	2. Turn off the light.	3. You spill a cup of hot coffee on yourself and on the floor. Clean it up.
4. Call up a friend and tell him or her you are sick.	5. Draw a picture of yourself on a piece of paper and hang it up on the wall.	6. Stand up. Put your hands on your head. Then sit down.
7. Cheer a classmate up.	8. Hand your phone number out to all the people in the group.	9. Take something out of your pocket and throw it away.
10. Take off an article of clothing and put it on someone else.	11. Turn on something electrical (CD player, printer, light, etc.) and then turn it off.	12. Pretend you find a word whose meaning you don't know. Look it up in the dictionary.

ACTIVITY 4 listening/speaking

■ **STEP 1** Listen to the conversation. Write down the problem.

Conversation 1: _____

Conversation 2: _____

Conversation 3: _____

■ **STEP 2** Listen to the conversation again, and complete the phrasal verbs you hear below:

Conversation 1: Turn _____   Turn _____   Put _____

Conversation 2: Clean _____   Fill _____   Put _____

Conversation 3: Figure _____   Call _____   Turn _____

■ **STEP 3** For each problem, add a solution of your own.

ACTIVITY 5 writing

■ **STEP 1** Work with a partner. Look back at the phrasal verbs in this unit. What phrasal verbs do you associate with the contexts below? Write them in the appropriate circle or redraw these circles in your notebook.

(At school)   (At home)   (At a party)

■ **STEP 2** Choose one of the contexts. Write a dialogue using as many phrasal verbs as you can.

ACTIVITY **6** research on the web

 Search the Internet for the meanings of the following phrasal verbs. Use a search engine such as Google® or Yahoo® or Ask® and enter the keywords: *dictionary* and *search* plus the phrasal verb. Write the meaning in the chart below. Then write a sentence that shows the change in meaning with each different particle.

		SENTENCE	MEANING
take	over		
	away		
	up		
look	over		
	into		
	up to		
give	out		
	into		
	back		

ACTIVITY **7** reflection

■ **STEP 1**   Give an example of a time when:

- communication broke down
- you figured out the meaning of a new word
- you felt frustrated and gave up

■ **STEP 2**   Explain what happened each time. What will you do next time?

Example: *I had a problem with my rent. I talked to my landlord on the phone. I didn't understand what he was saying. I was embarrassed, so I hung up the phone. Next time I'll let him I don't understand. I'll ask him to say it a different way.*

COMPARISON USING ADJECTIVES

UNIT GOALS

- Use the (regular and irregular) comparative form of adjectives in statements

- Ask questions using comparative adjectives

- Express similarities and differences with adjectives using *as . . . as*

- Make polite comparisons

OPENING TASK

Comparison Shopping for an Apartment

■ STEP 1

You are a college student looking for an apartment. Look at the two apartment ads and compare them using the adjectives on the next page.

FOR RENT

Studio Apartment. 400 square feet. Centrally located. Close to bus stop and downtown. Fully furnished. $800/ month plus utilities.

small

close to public transportation

far away from downtown

expensive

spacious

quiet

safe

new

sunny

furnished

▪ STEP 2

In your opinion, which apartment is better? Give reasons for your choice.

I think the _____ *is better because . . .*

form

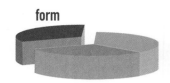

FOCUS 1 Comparative Form of Adjectives

Regular Comparatives

There are two regular comparative forms of adjectives in English.

1. For adjectives with one syllable or those ending in *–y*:

X *is* _____ *er than* Y.

EXAMPLE	ADJECTIVE	COMPARATIVE	RULE
(a) This neighborhood is **safer than** that one.	*safe*	*safer than*	For adjectives ending in -*e*, add -*r*.
(b) The one-bedroom apartment is **bigger than** the studio.	*big*	*bigger than*	For adjectives ending in consonant-vowel-consonant, double the consonant, add -*er*.
(c) The studio is **noisier than** the one bedroom.	*noisy*	*noisier than*	For adjectives ending in -*y*, change the -*y* to *i*, add -*er*.
(d) The studio is **smaller than** the one-bedroom.	*small*	*smaller than*	For all other adjectives, add -*er*.

2. For adjectives with two or more syllables:

X *is* (*more/less*) _____ *than* Y.

EXAMPLE	ADJECTIVE	COMPARATIVE	RULE
(e) The studio is **more economical than** the one-bedroom.	*economical*	*more economical than*	Use *more* or *less* before the adjective.
(f) The studio is **less expensive than** the one-bedroom.	*expensive*	*less expensive than*	

Notes

Some adjectives with two syllables can take either *-er* or *more/less*.	My apartment is **quieter than** yours. OR My apartment is **more quiet than** yours.
The forms we use in formal and informal English may be different.	In formal English we say: Joe is taller than **I** (am). In informal English we sometimes say: Joe is taller than **me**.
When you make a comparison, be sure to compare two **like** things.	**My hair** is longer than **Rita's (hair)**. NOT: **My hair** is longer than **Rita**.

Irregular Comparatives

EXAMPLES	EXPLANATIONS
(g) This neighborhood is **better than** that one.	The comparative forms of *good*, *bad*, and *far* are irregular.
(h) This year's winter was **worse than** last year's (winter).	*good—better*
(i) The one-bedroom is **farther** away from the bus stop **than** the studio is.	*bad—worse* *far—farther*
(j) This apartment is **much better than** that one.	Use *much* to make a comparison stronger.
(k) This apartment is **much farther than** the other one.	

EXERCISE 1

Complete the statements using the comparative form of each adjective in parentheses + *than*. Then make a logical conclusion for each set of sentences.

Examples: a. E-mail is (fast) ____faster than____ regular mail.
b. E-mail is (easy) ____easier than____ regular mail.
c. E-mail is (practical) _more practical than_ regular mail.

1. Online shoppers say:
   a. Shopping online is (convenient) _____ shopping in a department store.
   b. Shopping online is (relaxing) _____ shopping in a store.
   c. Therefore, shopping online is (good) _____ shopping in a store.

2. Small car owners say:
   a. Big cars are (difficult) _____ to drive _____ small cars.
   b. Big cars are (economical) _____ small cars.
   c. Therefore, big cars are (desirable) _____ small cars.

3. People who live in small towns say:
   a. Big cities are (crowded) _____ small towns.
   b. Big cities are (expensive) _____ small towns.
   c. Life in big cities is (difficult) _____ life in small towns.
4. Healthy people say:
   a. Fast food is (nutritious) _____ health food.
   b. Fast food is (fattening) _____ health food.
   c. Health food is (safe) _____ fast food.

EXERCISE 2

Fill in the blanks with the comparative form of the adjective.

Jane: Kevin, I found these two apartment ads in the newspaper this morning. There's a studio and a one-bedroom. I think the one-bedroom sounds nice. What do you think?

Kevin: Well, the one bedroom is definitely (1) (large) _____ than the studio, but the studio is (2) (cheap) _____. You know you only have a part-time job. How can you afford to pay $1,200 a month for rent?

Jane: I know the one-bedroom is (3) (expensive) _____, but I have so much furniture. The one-bedroom is (4) (big) _____ and I want to invite guests and it will be much (5) (comfortable) _____. Besides, maybe someday I'll have a roommate, and I'll need a (6) (spacious) _____ apartment, Kevin.

Kevin: Well, maybe, but you need to be realistic. The studio is in the center of town. You'll be (7) (close) _____ to transportation, stores, the library, and the college.

Jane: You're much (8) (practical) _____ than I am, Kevin. But the studio is directly over a nightclub, so it will be (9) (noisy) _____ than the one-bedroom. I will need peace and quiet so I can study.

Kevin: Listen—the studio is small, but it's much (10) (cozy) _____ than the one-bedroom and you'll spend much less time cleaning it!

Jane: True, but I think the one-bedroom will be much (11) (safe) _____ and (12) (good) _____ for me than the studio.

Kevin: It seems to me your mind is made up.

Jane: Yes, it is. By the way, Kevin, I'm going to see the one-bedroom later today. Can you come with me?

Kevin: Sure.

EXERCISE 3

Write an advertisement for each product on the left. In your advertisement, compare one product to the product on the right. Use the adjectives below.

Example: *Hassenflas Ice Cream tastes richer than Momma Millie's Frozen Yogurt.*

1. **Product:** Hassenflas Ice Cream
   Compare with: Momma Millie's Frozen Yogurt
   Adjectives: rich, creamy, delicious, sweet, fattening, healthy

_____

_____

_____

2. **Product:** Serenity Vacation Cruise
   Compare with: Adventure Package Vacation
   Adjectives: luxurious, expensive, enjoyable, relaxing, long, exciting, active, adventurous

_____

_____

_____

3. **Product:** Sportso Compact Car
   Compare with: Big Boy SUV
   Adjectives: fast, comfortable, fuel-efficient, safe, sporty, cheap, expensive

_____

_____

_____

EXERCISE 4

Miyuki wants to study English in the United States. She knows about an English program in Brattleboro, a small town in Vermont. She also knows about a program in Los Angeles, California. She needs to decide where she wants to live. Here is some information about the two places.

	BRATTLEBORO, VERMONT	LOS ANGELES, CALIFORNIA
1. rent for a one-bedroom apartment	$750 a month	$1,500 a month
2. population	12,000	3.8 million
3. weather	very cold in winter hot in summer	warm in winter hot in summer
4. public transportation	bus	bus, metro
5. quality of life		
a. air quality	clean	not so clean
b. the crime rate	1.7 crimes per 1,000 people	12.7 violent crimes per 1,000 people
c. lifestyle	quiet	exciting
d. traffic	light	heavy

Make comparative statements about Brattleboro and Los Angeles using the adjectives in parentheses.

1. crime rate (low/high) <u>The crime rate is lower in Brattleboro than in Los Angeles.</u>
<u>The crime rate is higher in Los Angeles than in Brattleboro.</u>

2. city (populated) _____

3. apartments (cheap/expensive) _____

4. public transportation (good/bad) _____

5. winters (cold) _____

6. city streets (dangerous/safe) _____

7. air (clean) _____

8. traffic (heavy/light) _____

9. lifestyle (quiet/exciting) _____

10. In your opinion, which place is better for Miyuki? Why?

_____

_____

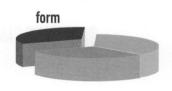

form

FOCUS 2 | Questions with Comparative Adjectives

EXAMPLES

Yes/No Questions

(a) **Are** private universities **more expensive than** public universities?

(b) **Are** private universities **better than** public universities?

(c) **Are** public universities **less expensive than** private universities?

Information (*Wh*-Questions)

(d) **Who** is **more serious** about school: you or your friend?

(e) **Which** is **more affordable:** a public university or a private university?

(f) **Whose** grades are **higher:** yours or your friend's?

EXERCISE 5

Refer to the Opening Task on pages 362–363 and ask a partner *yes/no* questions about the studio and the one-bedroom apartment. Answer the questions.

Example: economical

> **You:** *Is the studio more economical than the one-bedroom?*
> **Your partner:** *Yes, it is.*

1. practical
2. far from the downtown area
3. small
4. cheap
5. sunny
6. comfortable
7. economical
8. roomy
9. quiet
10. convenient
11. close to the bus stop
12. pretty
13. large
14. good

EXERCISE 6

Work with a partner. Interview each other about your impressions of the United States in comparison with your native country. Ask *yes/no* questions with the cues below.

Example: children in the United States/spoiled
> **You:** *Are children in the United States more spoiled than children in your country?*
> **Your partner:** *Yes, they are.* OR *No, they aren't.* OR *I'm not sure.*

1. people in the United States/friendly
2. educational opportunities/good
3. the cost of a college education in the United States/expensive
4. the American population/diverse
5. American citizens/safe
6. American food/tasty
7. Americans/happy
8. families in other countries/close
9. gasoline in the United States/cheap
10. Americans/generous
11. American women/independent
12. the divorce rate in the United States/high

EXERCISE 7

Ask a partner questions with *who, which,* or *whose* and the words in parentheses. Answer each other's questions.

Examples: (popular) *Who is more popular, Ricky Martin or Bono?*
> (practical) *Which is less practical, a regular phone or a cell phone?*

1. (wise) you or your parents?
2. (difficult) giving a speech or writing an essay English?
3. (hard) a man's life or a woman's life?
4. (bad) ironing or vacuuming?
5. (cheap) a public American university or a private American university?
6. (interesting) a taxicab driver's job or a scientist's job?
7. (delicious) vanilla or chocolate ice cream?
8. (dangerous) a motorcycle or a car?
9. (sensitive) a man or a woman?
10. (neat) your handwriting or your partner's handwriting?
11. (delicious) Chinese food or Italian food?
12. (spicy) Indian food or Thai food?

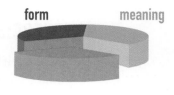

FOCUS 3

Expressing Similarities and Differences with *As . . . As*

EXAMPLES	EXPLANATIONS
(a) Mark is **as tall as** Sam. (b) Tokyo is **as crowded as** Seoul.	To say two things are equal or the same, use *as* + adjective + *as*.
(c) Mark isn't **as tall as** Steve. (= Steve is taller than Mark.) (d) A walkman isn't **as expensive as** an MP3 player.	To say there is a difference between two things, use *not as* + adjective + *as*.

EXERCISE 8

Read the conversation between Tommy and his mother about the choice between a car and a motorcycle. Write the correct form of the comparative in the blanks. Use *-er, more than, less than,* and *as . . . as*.

Mother: Tommy, I don't want you to buy a motorcycle. Why don't you buy a car instead? A car is (1) __more convenient than__ (convenient) a motorcycle, and it's (2) _____ (practical), too.

Tommy: Maybe it is, Mom, but a car isn't (3) _____ (economical) a motorcycle. I can get 50 miles to a gallon with a motorcycle! And a motorcycle's (4) _____ (cheap) a car.

Mother: Listen to me. You live in a big city. There are a lot of crazy people out there on the streets. A car is (5) _____ (safe) a motorcycle.

Tommy: Mom, I'm a good driver. I'm (6) _____ (good) you are! Besides that, it's (7) _____ (easy) to park a motorcycle in the city than it is to park a car.

Mother: Well, you're right about that.

Tommy: And all my friends are getting motorcycles, Mom. I won't look (8) _____ (cool) my friends.

Mother: I don't care, Tommy. Maybe their mothers aren't (9) _____ (nervous) I am. Let me think about it . . .

Tommy: Well, don't think about it too much, Mom . . . I'm already 35!!

EXERCISE 9

Work with a partner. You are selling Product #1, and your partner is selling Product #2. Make comparative statements using *–er, more than, less than,* and *as...as.* Try to make the most convincing advertisement!

Example: **You:** *Headstrong Headache Relief is **stronger than** Mogain Headache Relief.*
Your partner: *Headstrong Headache Relief is **not as strong as** Mogain Headache Relief.*

ADJECTIVES	PRODUCT 1	PRODUCT 2
1. effective stronger expensive fast-acting long-lasting	HEADSTRONG Headache Relief is ...	MOGAIN Headache Relief is ...
2. economical clean safe for the environment expensive fast	A hybrid car is ...	A gasoline-powered car is...
3. soft clean shiny natural-looking beautiful	SHIMMER Shampoo will leave your hair ...	GLIMMER Shampoo will ...
4. white bright clean healthy fresh	With SWISH toothpaste, your teeth will be ...	With SWIRL toothpaste, ...

EXERCISE 10

Look at the idiomatic expressions with comparisons. Then complete the sentences with one of the expressions below.

1. as snug as a bug in a rug.

2. as cool as a cucumber!

3. as busy as a bee!

4. as strong as an ox

5. as light as a feather

1. Look at that baby sleeping in his stroller. He's

   _____ .

2. How can you carry those heavy books to school every day? Don't worry. I'm

   _____ .

3. I'm sorry, John. I won't be able to have lunch with you today. I have so much to do.
   I'm _____ .

4. **Liz:** I think I need to go on a diet, Karen. I'm gaining weight.

   Karen: Are you crazy? You're _____!!!

5. I really admire our new boss. She always stays calm under stress. She's

   _____ .

use

FOCUS 4   Making Polite Comparisons

EXAMPLES	EXPLANATIONS
(a) Hamid is **shorter than** Marco. (b) Hamid is **not as tall as** Marco.	Sentence (b) is more polite. To make a polite comparison, use *not as* + adjective + *as*.

EXERCISE 11

Work in pairs. One student is "Blunt Betty." This person's statements are very direct and a little impolite. Read a statement from Column A. The other student, "Polite Polly," makes a statement with the same meaning, using *not as* + adjective + *as* to make the first statement more polite.

Column A: Blunt Betty	Column B: Polite Polly
1. Marco is fatter than Jonathan	(thin) Marco is not as thin as Jonathan.
2. Tom's watch is cheaper than Ray's.	(expensive)
3. Your handwriting is sloppier than mine.	(neat)
4. Henry's computer skills are worse than Jack's.	(good)
5. American coffee is weaker than Turkish coffee.	(strong)
6. Amy's neighborhood is more dangerous than Sarah's.	(safe)
7. Your apartment is smaller than ours.	(spacious)
8. Chris is sadder than his brother.	(happy)
9. Your child is lazier than mine.	(ambitious)
10. He is older than I am.	(young)

EXERCISE 12

Make true statements about yourself. Use each of the categories below. Add more categories of your own.

Examples: *My partner's older than I am. My partner's older than me.*
I'm not as old as he is. I'm not as old as him.

Categories	Me	My Partner
1. Age	19	24
2. Height		
3. Hair length		
4. Hair color		
5. Personality		
6. Other		

EXERCISE 13

Correct the errors in the following sentences.

1. John is more tall than Mary.

2. Seoul is more safer than Los Angeles.

3. Paul is as intelligent than Robert.

4. Mary is not beautiful as Kim.

5. My test scores were more worse than Margaret's.

6. Lorraine's eyes are darker than me.

7. Jeff is more handsomer than Jack.

8. My parents' life was hard than mine.

9. Is New York exciting as Paris?

10. Is Lake Ontario cleaner that Lake Erie?

11. The Hudson River is not polluted as the Volga River.

12. Mexico's capital city is more crowded than the United States.

13. My typing skills are faster than her.

Use Your English

ACTIVITY 1 speaking

How much do the following things cost in your country? In your notebook write the cost in U.S. dollars for each thing in your country. Ask a partner the prices of the same things in his or her country. Add three items of your own. Present your comparisons to the class. Example: *A gallon of gas is more expensive in Malaysia than in Indonesia.*

a gallon* of gas	a pair of jeans	rent for a one-bedroom apartment
a movie ticket	a cup of coffee	
a CD	cell phone service	
* one gallon = about 4 liters		

ACTIVITY 2 writing/speaking

Work in a group. Write six statements comparing cities, countries, or other places in the world. Make three statements that are true and three statements that are false. Read the statements to the class. The class decides if they are true or false.

Examples: *Canada is larger than the People's Republic of China.* (False)
The Pacific Ocean is bigger than the Atlantic Ocean. (True)

ACTIVITY 3 writing/speaking

Work with a partner. Find a product or service you want to sell. Create a name for it. Then create a print ad or a 30-second radio or TV commercial for the product or service. Present your ads or commercials to the class.

ACTIVITY 4 — research on the web

Search the Internet for the meaning of five of the idiomatic expressions listed below. Use a search engine such as Google® or Yahoo® or Ask® and enter the keywords: *meaning* and *phrase* plus the idiomatic expression. Find a picture on the Internet, or draw one to illustrate it.

Example: keywords: *"as cute as a button" meaning phrase*
Hint: Put idioms between quotation marks to search.

1. as cute as a button
2. as clean as a whistle
3. as easy as pie
4. as solid as a rock
5. as happy as a clam
6. as clear as day
7. as sick as a dog
8. as proud as a peacock
9. as fresh as a daisy
10. as good as gold

ACTIVITY 5 — listening/speaking

CD Track 21

■ **STEP 1**   Shelly is trying to decide what kind of computer to buy. Listen to her conversation with her friend Anna. List the advantages and disadvantages for the laptop and the desktop computers.

	ADVANTAGES	DISADVANTAGES
LAPTOP	more practical	harder to use
DESKTOP		

■ **STEP 2**   Work with a partner. Discuss which computer Shelly finally decides to buy and why? Do you agree with her?

COMPARISON USING ADVERBS

UNIT GOALS

- Use the (regular and irregular) comparative form of adverbs in statements

- Express similarities and differences with adverbs using *as . . . as*

- Ask questions with *how*

OPENING TASK

Differences Between Men and Women

Work in groups of three. Do men and women behave differently? Make a statement comparing men and women for each behavior below.

1. behave aggressively

    _____

2. drive safely

    _____

3. take risks confidently

    _____

4. work hard

    _____

5. teach children patiently

    _____

6. express their feelings openly

    _____

7. learn math easily

    _____

8. spend money freely

    _____

9. solve problems well

    _____

10. think clearly in emergencies

    _____

Talk about your answers with your classmates.

form

use

FOCUS 1 | Comparative Forms of Adverbs

EXAMPLE	ADVERB	COMPARATIVE	RULE
(a) Women live **longer than** men.	*long*	*longer than*	For short adverbs, add *-er* + *than*.
(b) Do women drive **more safely than** men?	*safely*	*more/less safely than*	For adverbs with two or more syllables, use *more/less* + adverb + *than*.
(c) Do men drive **less carefully than** women?	*carefully*	*more/less carefully than*	
(d) Men eat out much **more often than** women.	*often*	*more/less often than*	With adverbs of frequency, use *more/less* + adverb + *than*.
(e) Do women cook **better than** men?	*well*	*better than*	
(f) Do boys do **worse** in school **than** girls?	*badly*	*worse than*	With irregular adverbs, use the irregular form + *than*.
(g) Can a man throw a ball **farther than** a woman can?	*far*	*farther than*	

EXAMPLES	EXPLANATIONS
(h) Jason can climb higher than his sister **can**.	Sometimes, the auxiliary verb, for example *can* or *will*, follows the subject after *than*.
(i) She's better in school than I **am**.	*Be* can also follow the Subject after *than*.
(j) I type faster than my friend **does**. (k) We speak Spanish better than they **do**.	If there is no *be* or auxiliary verb, you can use *do*.
(l) I type faster than she **does**. (m) I type faster than **her**.	In formal English speech and writing, the subject pronoun follows *than*. In informal English speech, the object pronoun (*me, you, him, her, us, them*) sometimes follows *than*.

EXERCISE 1

Write statements comparing men and women for each behavior below.

Example: run fast

Men run faster than women (do).
_____

1. take care of elderly parents compassionately
_____

2. play games competitively
_____

3. drive aggressively
_____

4. make friends easily
_____

5. say "I love you" willingly
_____

EXERCISE 2

Work with a partner of the opposite sex, if possible. Write statements comparing yourself with your partner. Use the verbs and adverbs in the chart. Compare your answers with your classmates' answers. Do the men and women in your class behave differently?

VERB	ADVERB	COMPARISONS
1. cry	easily	My partner cries more easily than I (do).
2. listen to others	carefully	
3. watch sports on TV	frequently	
4. exercise	regularly	
5. ask for directions	willingly	
6. study	hard	
7. talk	freely	
8. participate in class	actively	
9. cook	well	
10. read maps	accurately	

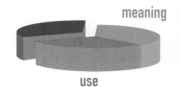

FOCUS 2 — Expressing Similarities and Differences with *As . . . As*

EXAMPLES	EXPLANATIONS
(a) A woman can work **as hard as** a man. (b) A man can dance **as gracefully as** a woman.	To show similarities, use *as* + adverb + *as*.
(c) He does**n't** speak **as clearly as** I (do). (d) = I speak more clearly than he (does). (e) = He speaks less clearly than I (do).	To show differences, use *not as* + adverb + *as*. Remember that (c) is more polite, more tactful than (d) or (e). (See Focus 4 in Unit 22 on page 374.)

▓ EXERCISE 3

Sally Miller and Bill Benson are applying for a job as director of an art company. Decide who is better for the job. Make comparative statements about each person.

Examples: *Sally works as hard as Bill.*
Bill draws better than Sally. / Sally doesn't draw as well as Bill.

WORK HABITS	SALLY MILLER	BILL BENSON
1. works hard	✔	✔
2. draws well		✔
3. thinks creatively	✔	✔
4. communicates openly	✔	
5. plans carefully		✔
6. works well with others	✔	✔
7. treats the staff fairly	✔	
8. solves problems successfully		✔
9. deals with clients tactfully	✔	✔
10. works efficiently		✔

EXERCISE 4

Imagine you are the president of the art company. You want to compare Sally and Bill. Write some questions to ask about their abilities.

Examples: *Does Sally work as hard as Bill?*
Does Bill draw better than Sally?

EXERCISE 5

Discuss these questions before you read.

1. Do you think boys and girls grow up differently?
   In what ways do they grow up differently?

2. Do you think boys and girls talk to each other differently?

3. Do you think boys and girls play differently? In what ways?

Now, read the following:

Boys and girls grow up in different worlds. Research studies show that boys and girls act very differently. For example, when children play, boys don't play with girls, and girls don't play with boys. Some of their activities are similar, but their favorite games are different. Also, the language they use in games is different.

Boys usually play outside in large groups. The group has a leader. The leader gives orders. There are winners and losers in boys' games. Boys frequently brag about how good they are at something and argue about who is the best.

Girls, on the other hand, play in small groups or pairs. The most important thing for a girl is her best friend. Closeness is very important to girls. Girls like to sit together and talk. In their games, like jump rope, everyone gets a turn. In many of their activities, such as playing together with their dolls, there are no winners or losers. Girls don't brag about how good they are at something. They don't give orders. They usually make suggestions.

Does this text match your answers to the three questions above? What information is the same? What information is different?

EXERCISE 6

To test your understanding of the reading, check *True* or *False* for the statements below.

	TRUE	FALSE
1. Boys and girls play differently.		
2. Boys and girls play together.		
3. Girls act more aggressively than boys.		
4. Girls play more competitively than boys do.		
5. Boys brag about how good they are at something more frequently than girls.		
6. Girls talk to each other more intimately than boys do.		
7. Girls give suggestions more readily than boys.		
8. Boys play more cooperatively than girls do.		
9. Girls play more fairly in their games than boys.		
10. Girls and boys speak to each other differently.		

EXERCISE 7

Read each statement aloud. For each statement you read, your partner says how he or she is similar or different.

Example: **You:** *I (can) cook well.*
   Your partner: *I can cook as well as you.*
   I can't cook as well as you.
   I can cook better than you.

1. speak clearly
2. dance gracefully
3. sing sweetly
4. jump high
5. run far
6. add numbers quickly
7. meet new people easily
8. tell a joke well
9. study hard
10. learn English independently

EXERCISE 8

Write statements comparing men and women. Use *more/less/as . . . as*. Add two statements of your own. Then discuss your answers with the class. The first one has been done for you.

1. think creatively
   Men think less creatively than women.
   Women think as creatively as men (do).

2. run fast

3. behave responsibly

4. grow up quickly

5. ask for directions willingly

6. listen supportively

7. act independently

8. think logically

9. make friends easily

10. take care of their parents better

11.

12.

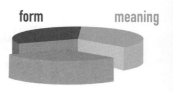

FOCUS 3   Questions with *How*

EXAMPLES	EXPLANATIONS
(a) **How old** are you? (b) **How well** do you speak English?	An adjective (*old, tall*) or an adverb (*well, far*) is often used in a *how* question.
(c) **How far** is it from here to the park? It's about five blocks.	*How far* asks about distance.
(d) **How long does it take** to fly from New York to Saigon? It takes about twenty-four hours. (e) **How long does it take** you to prepare dinner? It takes me an hour.	*How long does it take* asks about time.

EXERCISE 9

Ask a partner questions with *how*. Fill in your partner's answers on the right. Your partner asks you the same questions, and fills in your answers on the left.

Examples: *How far do you live from school?*
 How well can you cook?

	YOU	YOUR PARTNER
1. how far/live from school	5 miles	4 blocks
2. how well/cook	very well	very well
3. how easily/fall asleep at night		
4. how far/run		
5. how hard/study		
6. how fast/type		
7. how late/stay up at night		
8. how early/get up in the morning		
9. how well/know your classmates		
10. how often/speak to your best friend		

EXERCISE 10

Compare yourself with your partner for each of the questions in Exercise 9.

1. I live farther away from school than my partner (does).
2. My partner cooks as well as I (do).
3. _____.
4. _____.
5. _____.
6. _____.
7. _____.
8. _____.
9. _____.
10. _____.

EXERCISE 11

Fill in the chart. Say how much time it takes you to do each of the activities below. Then interview a partner. Say how long it takes you both to do these activities.

Examples: *It takes me longer to do my homework.*
I get dressed faster than you (do) in
the morning.

	YOU	YOUR PARTNER
1. do your homework	1 hour	45 minutes
2. get dressed in the morning		
3. get to school		
4. clean your room/apartment/house		
5. have breakfast		
6. take a shower		
7. cook dinner		
8. fall asleep at night		
9. read your e-mail every day		

Use Your English

ACTIVITY 1 writing

Write statements comparing two cities or places that you know. Add two sentences of your own.

Example: *The trains run more smoothly in Montreal than in New York.*

1. trains/run smoothly
2. buses/run efficiently
3. people/work hard
4. taxi drivers/drive recklessly
5. traffic/move slowly
6. people/talk fast
7. people/talk to foreigners readily
8. stores/stay open late
9. people/drive fast
10. families/take vacations frequently

ACTIVITY 2 writing

Compare yourself with someone you know—a family member, a friend, your boyfriend/girlfriend, etc. Write a paragraph with a topic sentence.

Example: *I am more emotional than my best friend. I cry more easily than she does. . . .*

■ **STEP 1**   Here is a list of adverbs and a list of actions. Write each adverb and each action on a separate card.

Adverbs	Actions
slowly	eat spaghetti
sadly	put on your clothes
nervously	make the bed
angrily	cook dinner
fast	write an e-mail
carefully	brush your teeth
seriously	comb your hair
happily	paint a picture
secretly	play tennis
enthusiastically	shake someone's hand
shyly	do exercise

■ **STEP 2**   Mix up each group of cards separately. With a partner, take one adverb card and one action card.

■ **STEP 3**   Both of you mime the same action and adverb. The class guesses the action and the adverb.

■ **STEP 4**   The class compares your two performances.

Example: angrily/eat spaghetti
Paola ate spaghetti more angrily than Maria.

ACTIVITY 4 speaking

Planning a Vacation

Here is a map of the southwestern
United States. You and your friend
want to take a two-week vacation to
visit four national parks. You will start
and end your trip in Las Vegas, Nevada.

Approximate Mileage Between National Parks and Las Vegas

	LAS VEGAS	BRYCE CANYON	DEATH VALLEY	GRAND CANYON	ZION NATIONAL PARK
Las Vegas	————	245	130	275	145
Bryce Canyon	(245)	————	365	300	100
Death Valley	130	365	————	405	275
Grand Canyon	275	300	405	————	250
Zion National Park	145	100	275	250	————

■ **STEP 1**

Use the map and the mileage chart. Ask each other questions to find
out the distances between parks. Fill in the information in the chart
below. **Example:** *How far is it from Las Vegas to Death Valley? It's 130 miles.*

DEPART FROM LAS VEGAS	DISTANCE	TIME
Stop 1: Death Valley	130 miles	2 hours
Stop 2: Zion National Park		
Stop 3: Bryce Canyon		
Stop 4: Grand Canyon		

■ **STEP 2**

Calculate the time required to go from one place to another, and fill
in the information in the chart. Remember you will travel by car,
and the average speed limit is 65 miles per hour. All distances are in
miles. Take turns asking and answering questions about travel time.

Example: *How long does it take to get from Las Vegas to Death Valley? It takes
about two hours.*

ACTIVITY **5** listening/speaking

CD Track
22

■ **STEP 1**   Imagine that you have a problem. Do you want to discuss your problem with a male or a female friend? Work in groups of three. Give reasons for your choice.

■ **STEP 2**   Listen to the conversation. Take notes on Iris and Josh's ideas about male and female friends.

■ **STEP 3**   Do a survey. Ask the question in Step 1 to four people outside of class and write down their answers. In class, compare all the answers you collected. Is there a difference between male and female friends when you have a problem?

ACTIVITY **6** reflection

Self-Assessment
Write statements comparing your language behavior now to your language behavior at the beginning of this course.

BEHAVIOR	COMPARATIVE STATEMENTS
use a dictionary frequently	
read slowly	
express my ideas simply	
make friends quickly	
participate actively in conversations	
express my personality easily	
speak confidently	
respond to others nervously	
read and write regularly	
ask questions timidly	
understand others well	
use the language comfortably	

UNIT GOALS

- Understand the meaning of superlatives

- Know how to form regular and irregular superlatives

- Express facts and opinions using the expression *one of the* + superlative + plural noun

OPENING TASK
Geo-Quiz

STEP 1

Check your knowledge of geography. Circle the correct answer. Then work with a partner and compare your answers.

1. Which is the largest ocean?
   a. Pacific   b. Atlantic   c. Indian
2. Which is the highest mountain in the world?
   a. Everest   b. K2   c. Kangchenjunga
3. Which is the most widely spoken language in the world?
   a. English   b. Hindi   c. Chinese
4. Which is the hottest place in the world?
   a. Australia   b. Israel   c. Ethiopia
5. Which is the tallest office building in the world?
   a. the Sears Tower (Chicago, U.S.A.)   b. the Taipei 101 (Taipei, Taiwan)
   c. the Petronas Tower (Kuala Lumpur, Malaysia)
6. Which is the biggest island in the world?
   a. Greenland   b. New Guinea   c. Borneo
7. Which is the longest river in the world?
   a. Amazon   b. Yangtze   c. Nile
8. Which is the wettest place in the world?
   a. Hawaii   b. India   c. Jamaica
9. Which is the most populated city in the United States?
   a. Los Angeles   b. Chicago   c. New York City
10. Which is the smallest state in the United States?
    a. Connecticut   b. Delaware   c. Rhode Island

STEP 2

Now write three similar questions. Quiz your classmates.

11. _____
12. _____
13. _____

FOCUS 1   Superlative

EXAMPLES	EXPLANATIONS
(a) **The tallest** building in the world is the Taipei 101 in Taiwan. (b) Rosa sings **the most beautifully** of all. (c) **The least expensive** food on the menu is a hamburger.	Superlatives compare one thing or person to all the others in a group. **Least** is the opposite of **most**.
(d) Dr. Diaz is the most respected teacher **at the school.** (e) George Washington University is the most expensive university **in the United States.** (f) Diane cooks the best **of all the chefs.**	Use prepositional phrases after superlatives to identify the group.

EXERCISE 1

Go back to the Opening Task on page 393. Underline all the superlative forms in the questions.

Example: *Which is <u>the largest</u> ocean?*

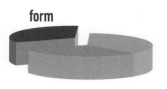

form

FOCUS 2 Regular and Irregular Superlative Forms

Regular Forms

EXAMPLES	ADJECTIVE	ADVERB	SUPERLATIVE FORM	RULE
(a) The Sears Tower in Chicago is **the tallest** building in the United States.	*tall*		*the tallest*	One-syllable adjectives or adverbs: *the* + adjective/adverb + *-est*
(b) My grandfather worked **the hardest** of his three brothers.		*hard*	*the hardest*	
(c) Jupiter is **the largest** planet.	*large*		*the largest*	One-syllable adjectives or adverbs ending in *-e:* add *-st.*
(d) I get up **the latest** in my family		*late*	*the latest*	
(e) **The hottest** place in the world is Ethiopia.	*hot*		*the hottest*	One-syllable adjectives ending in consonant-vowel-consonant: double the final consonant, add *-est.*
(f) **The easiest** subject for me is geography.	*easy*		*the easiest*	Two-syllable adjectives or adverbs ending in *-y:* change *-y* to *-i*; add *-est.*
(g) She arrived **the earliest.**		*early*	*the earliest*	
(h) **The most nutritious** fruit is the avocado.	*nutritious*		*the most nutritious*	Adjectives or adverbs with two or more syllables: use *the* + *most/least.*
(i) **The least expensive** food on the menu is a hamburger.	*expensive*		*the least expensive*	
(j) Of all his friends, he drives **the most carefully.**		*carefully*	*the most carefully*	
(k) She danced **the least gracefully** of all the students.		*gracefully*	*the least gracefully*	

Common Irregular Forms

ADJECTIVE	SUPERLATIVE	ADVERB	SUPERLATIVE
He is a **good** dancer.	He is **the best** dancer of the group.	He dances **well**.	He dances **the best** of all.
That was a **bad** movie.	That was **the worst** movie I saw last year.	She acts **badly**.	She acts **the worst** of all the actors.
The station is **far**.	That station is **the farthest**.	He ran **far**.	He ran **the farthest**.

EXERCISE 2

Here are some interesting facts from the *Guinness Book of World Records.* Write the superlative form of the adjective in parentheses in the blanks.

Example: (cold) Antarctica is ____the coldest____ place on earth.

1. _____ (large) pizza was 122 feet and 8 inches and was made in South Africa in 1990.

2. _____ (successful) pop group of all time was the Beatles.

3. _____ (heavy) baby at birth was a boy of 22 pounds, 8 ounces. He was born in Italy in 1955.

4. _____ (fat) person was a man in Seattle. He weighed almost 1,400 pounds.

5. _____ (productive) painter was Pablo Picasso. He produced about 13,500 paintings, 100,000 prints, 34,000 book illustrations, and 300 sculptures.

6. _____ (long) attack of hiccups lasted sixty-eight years.

7. _____ (big) omelet was made of 160,000 eggs in Yokohama, Japan, in 1994.

8. _____ (hot) city in the United States is Key West, Florida.

9. _____ (active) volcano in the world is Kilauea, on Hawaii.

10. _____ (old) man in the world was from Japan. He was 120 years and 237 days old.

EXERCISE 3

Information Gap. Work with a partner. One person looks at Chart A below, and the other person looks at Chart B on page A-21. Ask your partner questions to find out the missing information in your chart. Write the answers in the chart.

Example: Student A: *What is the longest river in North America?*
Student B: *The Mississippi.*

Chart A

	NORTH AMERICA	SOUTH AMERICA	ASIA	EUROPE	AFRICA	THE WORLD
long river		The Amazon		The Volga		The Nile
large country	Canada		The People's Republic of China		Sudan	
populated country		Brazil		Russia		The People's Republic of China
high mountain	Mt. McKinley		Mt. Everest		Mt. Kilimanjaro	
small country		Suriname		Vatican City		Vatican City

EXERCISE 4

Express your own opinion. Fill in the name of a student in your class and the superlative form of each adverb.

	Name		Adverb	Superlative
1.	Juan	does his homework	(carefully)	the most carefully .
2.	_____	writes	(well)	_____ .
3.	_____	arrives in class	(early)	_____ .
4.	_____	guesses new words	(fast)	_____ .
5.	_____	makes us laugh	(often)	_____ .
6.	_____	expresses opinions	(open)	_____ .
7.	_____	communicates in English	(effectively)	_____ .
8.	_____	participates in class	(actively)	_____ .
9.	_____	raises his/her hand	(frequently)	_____ .
10.	_____	works	(hard)	_____ .

Add two statements of your own.

11. _____ .

12. _____ .

EXERCISE 5

Play this game in two teams. Look at the game board on the next page. Choose one student from each team to come to the front of the room and act as questioner. Team 1 chooses a category and a dollar amount. The questioner from the other team asks the question with the superlative. Team 1 has one minute to choose an answer from the Answer Box. If the answer is correct, they "win" the money. If the answer is not correct, Team 2 answers the question and wins the money. The team with the most money at the end wins.

Example: **Team 1:** *"Animals" for $20.*
Reader: *dangerous animal: "What is the most dangerous animal?"*
Team 1: *The most dangerous animal is the mosquito. (Some mosquitoes carry malaria and other diseases that kill many people each year.)*

Gameboard

AWARD	PLANETS	ANIMALS	OTHER
$10			
$20			
$30			
$40			
$50			

Categories

Planets

$10 large planet/in the solar system?
$20 hot planet/in the solar system?
$30 close planet/to the Sun?
$40 light planet/in the solar system?
$50 close planet/to Earth?

Animals

$10 tall animal?
$20 dangerous animal?
$30 fast land animal?
$40 valuable animal?
$50 large and heavy animal?

Other

$10 cold place/on Earth?
$20 large desert/in the world?
$30 high court/in the United States?
$40 old mountain range/in the world?
$50 short day/of the year?

Answer Box (Choose the answers to the questions from this box.)

PLANETS	ANIMALS	OTHER
Neptune	the mosquito	the Supreme Court
Mercury	the blue whale	the Sahara
Venus	giraffe	the winter solstice (first day of winter)
Jupiter	cheetah	Antarctica
Saturn	race horse	the Urals

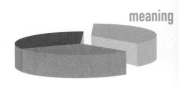

FOCUS 3 | *One of the* + Superlative + Plural Noun

EXAMPLES	EXPLANATION
(a) Bach was one of the greatest composers of all time. (There are several composers we think of as the greatest composers of all time. Bach is one of them.)	*One of the* + **superlative** + **plural noun** • is common with the superlative form • means that there are several people or things in a group we see as the best or worst. The people or things we are talking about are part of this group.
(b) Tim is one of the least popular students in the school. (There are several students we think of as the least popular students in the school. Tim is one of them.)	

EXERCISE 6

Fill in the blanks with *one of the* + superlative + plural noun. Use the words in parentheses. Then check *Fact* or *Opinion* for each statement.

Example: A Rolls Royce is <u>one of the most expensive cars</u> you can buy. (expensive car)

                                                             FACT   **OPINION**

1. Ice hockey is _____ you can play. (exciting sport)

2. Graduation was _____ of my life. (proud moment)

3. The Four Seasons is _____ in the United States. (expensive hotel)

4. Drinking and driving is _____ you can do. (bad thing)

5. The Guggenheim in Bilbao, Spain, is _____ in the world. (good museum)

6. Dr. Jones is _____ in the hospital. (fine doctor)

7. Louis Armstrong was _____ in America. (great jazz musicians)

8. This is _____ in the museum. (beautiful sculpture)

9. The tsunami in Asia in 2004 was _____ in history. (tragic natural disaster)

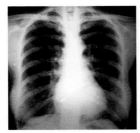

10. Heart disease is _____ in the United States. (high cause of death)

■ EXERCISE 7

Make statements with *one of the* + superlative + plural noun. Compare your opinions with your classmates' opinions.

Example: 1. *Prague is one of the most beautiful cities in the world.*

1. a beautiful city in the world
2. an interesting place (in the place you are living in)
3. a good restaurant (in the place you are in)
4. a famous leader in the world today
5. a deadly disease of our time
6. a serious problem in the world
7. a popular food (in the country you come from)
8. a funny show on television
9. a difficult language to learn
10. a dangerous career
11. a useful electronic device
12. an expensive city in the world

Use Your English

ACTIVITY  1 writing/speaking

Write ten questions to ask another student in the class about his or her home country or a country he or she knows. Use the superlative form of the words below, or add your own to the chart.

Examples: *What's the most crowded city in your country?*
What's the most popular sport in your country?
What's the most unusual food in your city?
Who's the most famous person in your country?

crowded city	popular sport	common food	hot month	important holiday
polluted city	expensive sport	unusual food	big problem	highly paid job
beautiful city	big city	popular music	famous person	popular vacation spot

ACTIVITY 2 speaking

In groups, discuss the following opinions. Tell your group if you agree or disagree and explain why.

1. Money is the most important thing in life.
2. AIDS is the worst disease in the world today.
3. English is the most difficult language to learn.
4. Poverty is the biggest problem in the world today.
5. Democracy is the best form of government.

ACTIVITY 3 — speaking

Interview a partner about his or her life experience. Use the adjectives below to write questions with superlatives. Tell the class about the most interesting things you learned about your partner.

Examples: *What was the best experience you had this year?*
What was the most embarrassing moment in your life?

unusual	sad	exciting
embarrassing	interesting	frightening
happy	dangerous	beautiful
funny	good	bad

ACTIVITY 4 — research on the web

Many of the facts in this unit are from the *Guinness Book of World Records.* Go to a search engine such as Google® or Yahoo® or Ask®, and enter the keywords: *Guinness Book of World Records.* Find five facts that have superlatives, such as the oldest person or the highest mountain on earth, and write them in your notebook. Compare your facts with those of other students in the class. Choose the most interesting or the most unusual facts.

ACTIVITY 5 — writing

Write a paragraph on one of the topics below:

    a. The most embarrassing moment in my life.

    b. The most frightening moment in my life.

    c. The funniest moment in my life.

ACTIVITY 6 listening/speaking

CD Track 23

■ **STEP 1** Listen to the quiz show. Circle the letter of the correct answer.

Quiz Choices:

1. a. North America b. Asia c. Africa
2. a. the elephant b. the turtle c. the bear
3. a. banana b. avocado c. orange
4. a. Chinese b. French c. English
5. a. North America b. Asia c. Antarctica
6. a. The United States b. China c. Canada
7. a. ruby b. diamond c. emerald
8. a. The Himalayas b. The Andes c. The Rockies
9. a. Spain b. The United States c. Italy
10. a. Van Gogh's b. Leonardo da Vinci's c. Rembrandt's *Self*
    Sunflowers   *Mona Lisa*   *Portrait*

■ **STEP 2** Discuss your answers with your classmates.

ACTIVITY 7 reflection

■ **STEP 1** What is the most challenging skill for you in English? Circle one
answer and explain why. Write your explanation on the line below.

a. Listening   b. Speaking   c. Reading   d. Writing

_____

■ **STEP 2** Read the list of language learning strategies for the **one** language
skill you said was the most challenging for you. Rate how
frequently you use these strategies. Then talk to a partner. Compare
the strategies you use for the skills you chose. Give each other
advice about how to be a better language learner.

LISTENING	NEVER	SOMETIMES	FREQUENTLY	THE MOST FREQUENTLY
Use my own knowledge to understand meaning				
Hear words and sentences clearly				
Make predictions				
Guess meaning in context				
Get the global meaning first				
Check my comprehension while listening				
Listen more than once				
Ask the speaker questions				
Don't worry if you don't understand every word				
SPEAKING	NEVER	SOMETIMES	FREQUENTLY	THE MOST FREQUENTLY
Use words from my native language				
Rehearse what I want to say before speaking				
Listen and try to imitate correct English pronunciation				
Think about grammar when speaking				
Try my best to express my meaning				
Use body language				
Ask others for help				
Don't worry about making errors				
Learn expressions, idioms, routines for conversation				

READING	NEVER	SOMETIMES	FREQUENTLY	THE MOST FREQUENTLY
Use my own knowledge to understand meaning				
Look at the text to get the global meaning first				
Think of questions I want the text to answer				
Guess meaning in context				
Use a dictionary				
Make predictions				
Check my comprehension while reading				
Re-read when necessary				
Don't worry if you don't understand every word				
WRITING	**NEVER**	**SOMETIMES**	**FREQUENTLY**	**THE MOST FREQUENTLY**
Take time to think and get ideas for writing first				
Think about who will read my writing				
Understand how writers organize their thinking				
Read a lot				
Try my best to express my meaning				
Be ready to revise / re-write				
Learn to check my writing				
Learn useful phrases for connecting ideas				
Ask others for help				

FACTUAL CONDITIONALS

If

UNIT GOALS

UNIT GOALS

- Use factual conditionals to express relationships that are always true and never change

- Use factual conditionals to express relationships based on habit

- Understand the order of clauses in factual conditionals

OPENING TASK

Test Your Knowledge of Science:
What do you know about water?

STEP 1

Work in groups of three. Complete each statement with a scientifically correct answer.

1. If you heat water to 212°F, it _____
2. If you cool water to 32°F, it _____
3. When you boil water, it _____
4. When water freezes, it _____
5. When you put an ice cube in a glass of water, the ice cube _____
6. When you add sugar to water, the sugar _____
7. Water boils faster when you _____
8. You cannot survive if you _____

STEP 2

Reread each statement in Step 1, and choose the correct answer from below.

a. don't have water
b. expands (gets bigger)
c. freezes
d. dissolves
e. boils
f. turns into a gas
g. floats
h. are at a high altitude (height above sea level)

How many did you answer correctly?

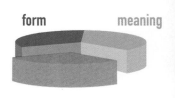

FOCUS 1 | Expressing Relationships That Never Change

Factual conditionals express relationships that are always true and never change. This type of conditional is often used in scientific writing.

EXAMPLES		EXPLANATIONS
Clause 1 (*If* Clause)	**Clause 2** (Main Clause)	
(a) If you heat water to 212° (degrees) Fahrenheit,	it boils.	Use the simple present in both clauses.* Place a comma after the *if* clause.
(b) If you don't water a house plant,	it dies.	
(c) When (ever) you add sugar to water,	the sugar dissolves.	You can use *when* or *whenever* in place of *if*. Also add a comma after the *when* (*ever*) clause.

* Note: A **clause** is a group of words containing a subject and verb which forms part of a sentence.

EXERCISE 1

Circle the correct medical answer.

Example:

1. If you eat too much salt,
   a. your blood pressure goes down.
   b. your blood pressure goes up.

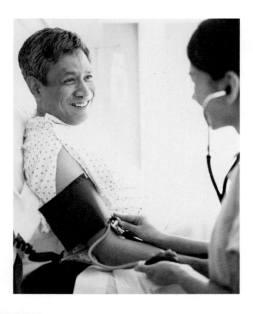

1. If you eat too much,

   a. you lose weight.

   b. you gain weight.

2. If you smoke,

   a. your health suffers.

   b. your health improves.

3. If you stay in the sun a lot,

   a. your skin stays young and smooth.

   b. your skin looks old faster.

4. If you wash your hands often,

   a. you get sick more frequently.

   b. you get sick less frequently.

5. If you brush your teeth every day,

   a. you get cavities.

   b. you prevent cavities.

6. If you don't sleep enough,

   a. you have a lot of energy.

   b. you feel tired.

7. When you get a flu shot,

   a. you protect yourself against the flu.

   b. you get the flu.

8. If you don't exercise regularly,

   a. your muscles become stronger.

   b. your muscles become weaker.

9. If you listen to loud music regularly,

   a. your hearing becomes worse.

   b. your hearing becomes better.

10. When you feel depressed in winter,

    a. bright light makes you sadder.

    b. bright light makes you happier.

EXERCISE 2

Test your knowledge about food and health. Find the *If* clause below that correctly completes each statement. Write the clause in the correct box. Discuss your answers with a partner.

If Clauses

a. If you eat different-colored fruits and vegetables,
b. If you eat small amounts of chocolate,
c. If you eat 3,200 extra calories,
d. If you don't get enough calcium in your diet,
e. When you go on a low-calorie diet,
f. If you eat too much sugar and too many fats and carbohydrates,

1. _____ you gain one pound.

2. _____ you can increase your risk for having diabetes.

3. _____ your bones get weak.

4. _____ your body thinks you are starving; so your body uses up calories more slowly.

5. _____ you can prevent cancer and heart disease.

6. _____ you feel happier and stay healthy.

EXERCISE 3

Proverbs are statements that express basic truths. Read the proverbs below. Discuss the meaning of each proverb with a partner. Then, rewrite each proverb as a factual conditional statement.

Example: The early bird catches the worm. _____ If you get up early, you succeed. _____

1. Practice makes perfect. _____

2. An apple a day keeps the doctor away. _____

3. Too many cooks spoil the broth. _____

4. Out of sight, out of mind. _____

5. Absence makes the heart grow fonder. _____

6. Easy come, easy go. _____

FOCUS 2 — Expressing Relationships Based on Habit

EXAMPLES

Clause 1 (*If* Clause)	Clause 2 (Main Clause)
(a) If I cook,	my husband **washes** the dishes.
(b) If I lied,	my mother **punished** me.
(c) When (ever) it **snowed,**	we **stayed** home from school.

EXPLANATIONS

Factual conditionals also express present or past habitual relationships. Habitual conditionals are common in everyday conversation. Use the same tense in both clauses.

You can use *when* or *whenever* in place of *if*.

EXERCISE 4

Make sentences with *if, when,* or *whenever.* Use the words in bold below or your own words in the main clause. Say your sentences aloud and compare your answers.

Example: you take a vacation every year/feel
If you take a vacation every year, you feel happy and refreshed.

1. you never take a vacation/**feel**
2. you have elderly parents/**worry**
3. you live with a roommate/**share**
4. you don't pay your credit card bill on time/**pay**
5. you exercise regularly/**stay**
6. someone sneezes/**say**
7. you don't want to cook/**eat**
8. you don't own a car/**use**

EXERCISE 5

In some cultures, people say, "If you find a four-leaf clover, you have good luck." We call these kinds of statements "old wives' tales." They are not always true, but people believe them and repeat them. Read the following "old wives' tales," and decide in your group if they are true or not.

1. If you go outside with wet hair, you catch a cold.
2. If your ears are ringing, someone is talking about you.
3. If you eat chicken soup, your cold gets better.
4. If you hold your breath, your hiccups go away.
5. If you eat spinach, you get big and strong.
6. If you break a mirror, you have seven years of bad luck.
7. If children drink coffee, they don't grow tall.
8. If you go swimming right after you eat, you can get cramps and drown.

Now add a few old wives' tales from your home country and tell your group about them.

EXERCISE 6

Complete the *if/whenever* clauses with a statement of your own.

Example: If I feel very tired when I come home, _____ I take a nap for ten minutes. _____

1. Whenever I can't fall asleep, _____.
2. Whenever I get angry, _____.
3. If I get a headache, _____.
4. If I am late for an appointment, _____.
5. If I gain weight, _____.
6. If I fail an exam, _____.
7. Whenever I have money to spend, _____.
8. If I eat too much, _____.
9. If I get very worried, _____.
10. Whenever I feel blue, _____.
11. Whenever I have a day off, _____.
    Add two statements of your own:
12. _____.
13. _____.

EXERCISE 7

Think of the definition for each word in italics. Find the phrase on the right that completes each statement. Say your statements aloud.

1. If you live in a *democracy,* you can
2. If you're *patient,* you don't
3. If you're a *night owl,* you
4. If you're a *teenager,* you
5. If you're a *member of the faculty,* you
6. If you're a *pediatrician,* you
7. If you're a *blue-collar worker,* you may
8. If you're *broke,* you don't
9. If you're a *shopaholic,* you
10. If you're *polylingual,* you
11. If you're an *introvert,* you
12. If you're an *early bird*, you

a. want to be independent.
b. go to bed late.
c. teach in a school or college.
d. lose your temper.
e. work in a factory.
f. have any money.
g. treat sick children.
h. vote in elections.
i. get up early in the morning.
j. love to buy things.
k. speak more than two languages.
l. like to be alone or with a few friends/family members.

EXERCISE 8

Work with a partner. Ask each other questions about your childhood. Then, compare your different childhoods.

Example: told a lie
  You: *When you were a child, what happened if you told a lie?*
  Your partner: *If I told a lie, my mother yelled at me.*

1. got sick
2. disobeyed your parents
3. did well in school
4. got a bad grade on your report card
5. came home very late
6. had a serious personal problem
7. fought with your brother or sister
8. got into a fight with a classmate
9. had a bad dream

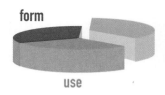

FOCUS 3 Order of Clauses in Factual Conditionals

EXAMPLES	EXPLANATIONS
(a) **If you study hard,** you get good grades.	The *if* clause is usually first.
(b) How do you get an A in this class? You get an A **if you do all the work.**	When the *if* clause contains new information, the *if* clause can be second. When it is second, there is no comma between the two clauses.
(c) How do you get extra credit? You get extra credit **when(ever) you do extra work.**	With *when* or *whenever,* you can also change the order of the clauses.

EXERCISE 9

Answer the questions below.

Example: When do you feel nervous?
I feel nervous if I have many things to do and little time.
I feel nervous whenever I have a test.

1. When do you feel nervous?
2. When do you get a headache?
3. How do you catch a cold?
4. When do you have trouble sleeping?
5. When did your parents punish you?
6. When were your parents pleased with you?
7. When do you get angry?
8. When do you feel excited?
9. How do you know if you're in love?
10. When do you miss home/feel homesick?
11. When do you feel disappointed?

Use Your English

ACTIVITY 1 writing/speaking

Psychologists say there are two personality types: A and B. *Type A* people worry, get nervous, and are under stress all the time. *Type B* people are calm and try to enjoy life.

■ **STEP 1**   Which personality type are you? Complete the statements.

   1. Whenever there is a change in my life, I . . .

   2. If I have a test, I . . .

   3. When I get stuck in traffic, I . . .

   4. When I enter a room with people I don't know, I . . .

   5. When another driver on the road makes a mistake, I . . .

   6. If a friend hurts my feelings, I . . .

   7. If I don't hear from my family and friends, I . . .

   8. When I have a lot of things to do in one day, I . . .

   9. When I don't succeed at something, I . . .

   10. When someone criticizes me, I . . .

■ **STEP 2**   Discuss your results in your group. Decide which students in the group are *Type A* personalities and which are *Type B*. Explain why. Make a chart in your notebook like the one below. Fill it in with your group's information.

NAME	TYPE A PERSONALITY	NAME	TYPE B PERSONALITY	
Stefan	If he has a test, he worries a lot. When he doesn't succeed at something, he gets angry at himself.			

FACTUAL CONDITIONALS *If*   417

ACTIVITY 2 writing/speaking

Do you have any unusual habits or problems eating certain foods? Make a list. Share your list of unusual habits with your group. Try to find the person with the most unusual habits.

Examples: *Whenever I feel anxious, I clean my closets.*
If I eat chocolate, I get a headache.

ACTIVITY 3 writing

Think about your childhood. Write five factual conditional statements about past habits or behaviors in your childhood.

Examples: *If my sister hit me, I hit her back.*
Whenever it snowed, we stayed home from school.

ACTIVITY 4 listening/speaking

CD Track 24

About 70 percent of Americans have problems sleeping. Listen to some recommendations from the National Sleep Foundation. As you listen, match each recommendation to a statement with the same meaning.

Recommendation 1: _____

Recommendation 2: _____

Recommendation 3: _____

Recommendation 4: _____

Recommendation 5: _____

a. Create a restful place to sleep.

b. Go to sleep only when you feel sleepy.

c. Cut down on drinks with caffeine.

d. Keep regular hours.

e. Develop a sleep routine.

ACTIVITY 5 speaking

■ **STEP 1**

Work in a group of four. Compare customs in different countries. Write the name of a country in the left column, and complete the main clause for each *if/when(ever)* clause.

Example: *In Italy, when you have dinner in a restaurant, you leave a tip.*

COUNTRY	IF/WHEN(EVER) CLAUSE	MAIN CLAUSE
Italy	you have dinner in a restaurant	you leave a tip
	someone gives you a compliment	
	someone gives you a gift	
	you greet an old friend	
	you greet an older person	
	a baby is born	
	someone sneezes	
	someone invites you to dinner	
	you want to refuse someone's invitation	

■ **STEP 2**

Add two more customs to the list and make statements about them.

ACTIVITY 6 reflection

Discuss the following with a partner.
What do you do when . . . .

a. **you are reading a text in English and**
   - you don't understand some of the vocabulary?
   - you don't get the main idea?
   - you don't know anything about the topic?

b. **you are having a conversation with someone and**
   - you don't understand what he/she is saying?
   - you can't express what you want to say?
   - he or she doesn't understand you?

c. **you are watching TV or a movie and**
   - you don't understand what someone is saying?

d. **you are speaking to someone and**
   - you don't know the word for something in English?
   - you don't know how to express your idea in English?
   - you are afraid your pronunciation is bad?

e. **you are writing and**
   - you don't have any ideas to write about?
   - you don't have enough vocabulary to write?
   - you don't know how to organize your writing?

ACTIVITY 7 research on the web

Many of our beliefs about food are based on "myths." You can find examples of food "myths" below:

> If you eat bread and other carbohydrates, you gain weight.
> If you eat eggs and red meat, you have heart problems.
> If you eat grapefruit, you burn calories.

■ STEP 1   Work in groups of three. Use a search engine such as Google® or Ask® or Yahoo®. Type in "the truth about food myths" or "food myths debunked." Find three food myths and read about them. Write each myth in the same type of sentence as the examples above (using Factual Conditionals.) Then explain in writing why they are not true.

■ STEP 2   Share what you've learned about these three food myths with your classmates.

Appendices

Appendix 1A *Be:* Present Tense

I	am	
He She It	is	from Japan.
We You They	are	
There	is	a student from Japan in our class.
There	are	students from all over the world in this class.

Appendix 1B *Be:* Past Tense

I He She It	was	happy.
We You They	were	
There	was	a party yesterday.
There	were	a lot of people there.

Appendix 1C   Simple Present

I You We They	work.
He She It	works.

Appendix 1D   Present Progressive

I	am	
He She It	is	working.
We You They	are	

Appendix 1E   Simple Past

I He She It We You They	worked	yesterday.

Appendix 1F   Future Tense with *Will*

I He She It We You They	will work	tomorrow.

Appendix 1G Future Tense with *Be Going To*

I	am	
He She It	is	going to work in a few minutes.
We You They	are	

Appendix 1H *Can/Might/May*

I He She It We You They	can might may	work.

Appendix 1I *Be Able To*

I	am	
He She It	is	able to dance.
We You They	are	

Appendix 2A Plural Nouns

NOUNS	SINGULAR	PLURAL
Regular	book	books
	table	tables
Ends in vowel +*y*	toy	toys
Ends in vowel +*o*	radio	radios
Ends in consonant +*o*	potato	potatoes
	tomato	tomatoes
Ends in consonant +*y*	city	cities
Ends in -*f* or -*fe*	thief	thieves
	wife	wives
(Except)	chief	chiefs
	chef	chefs
Ends in -*ss*, -*ch*, -*sh*, -*x*, or -*z*	class	classes
	sandwich	sandwiches
	dish	dishes
	box	boxes
Irregular plural nouns	man	men
	woman	women
	child	children
	foot	feet
	tooth	teeth
	mouse	mice
Plurals that stay the same	sheep	sheep
	deer	deer
	fish	fish
No singular form		scissors
		pants
		shorts
		pajamas
		glasses
		clothes

Appendix 2B   Simple Present: Third Person Singular

RULE	EXAMPLE
1. Add -*s* to form the third person singular of most verbs.	My brother **sleeps** 8 hours a night.
2. Add -*es* to verbs ending in -*sh*, -*ch*, -*x*, -*z*, or -*ss*.	She **watches** television every evening.
3. When the verb ends in a consonant +*y*, change the *y* to *i* and add -*es*.	He **hurries** to class every morning.
4. When the verb ends in a vowel +*y*, do not change the *y*. Add -*s*.	My sister **plays** the violin.
5. Irregular Forms: have go do	 He **has** a good job. He **goes** to work every day. He **does** the laundry.

Appendix 2C   Present Progressive

1. Add -*ing* to the base of the verb.	talk study do agree	talking studying doing agreeing
2. If the verb ends in a single -*e*, drop the -*e* and add -*ing*.	drive	driving
3. If a one-syllable verb has a consonant, a vowel, and a consonant (c-v-c), double the last consonant and add -*ing*.	(c-v-c) sit run	 sitting running
Do not double the consonant if the verb ends in -*w*, -*x*, or -*y*.	show fix play	showing fixing playing
4. In two-syllable verbs that end in a consonant, a vowel, and a consonant (c-v-c), double the last consonant only if the last syllable is stressed.	beGIN LISten	beginning listening
5. If the verb ends in -*ie*, drop the -*ie*, add -*y* and -*ing*.	lie die	lying dying

Appendix 2D Simple Past of Regular Verbs

Rule		
1. Add -ed to most regular verbs.	start	started
2. If the verb ends in an -e, add -d.	like	liked
3. If the verb ends in a consonant +y, change the y to i and add -ed.	study	studied
4. If the verb ends in a vowel +y, don't change the y to i. Add -ed.	enjoy	enjoyed
	play	played
5. If a one-syllable verb ends in a consonant, a vowel, and a consonant (c-v-c), double the last consonant and add -ed.	stop	stopped
	show	showed
Do not double the last consonant if it is w, x, or y.	fix	fixed
	play	played
6. If a two-syllable word ends in a consonant, a vowel, and a consonant (c-v-c), double the last consonant if the stress is on the last syllable.	ocCUR	occurred
	LISten	listened

APPENDIX 3 Pronunciation Rules

Appendix 3A Regular Plural Nouns

/S/	/Z/		/IZ/
After voiceless sounds (p, t, k, f, th)	After voiced sounds (b, d, g, v, m, n, l, r, ng) and vowel sounds		After s, z, sh, ch, ge/dge sounds. (This adds another syllable to the word.)
maps	jobs	pens	classes
pots	beds	schools	exercises
books	rugs	cars	dishes
cuffs	leaves	rings	sandwiches
months	rooms	days	colleges

Appendix 3B   Simple Present Tense: Third Person Singular

/S/	/Z/	/IZ/
After voiceless sounds (*p, t, k, f*)	After voiced final sounds (*b, d, g, v, l, r, m, n, ng*)	Verbs ending in *sh, ch, z, s*. (This adds another syllable to the word.)
He sleeps.	She drives a car.	He teaches English.
She works.	He prepares dinner.	She rushes to class.

Appendix 3C   Simple Past Tense of Regular Verbs

/t/	/d/	/Id/
After voiceless sounds (*p, k, f, s, sh, ch*)	After voiced final sounds (*b, g, v, l, r, m, n*)	Verbs ending in -*t* or -*d*. (This adds another syllable to the word.)
He kissed her once.	We learned a song.	She painted a picture.
She asked a question.	They waved goodbye.	The plane landed safely.

APPENDIX 4   Time Expressions

Appendix 4A   Simple Present

ADVERBS OF FREQUENCY	FREQUENCY EXPRESSIONS	TIME EXPRESSIONS
always	morning	in { 1997 / October / the fall
often	afternoon	
frequently	night	
usually	summer	on { Monday / Sundays / January 1st / the weekend
sometimes	every { winter	
seldom	spring	
rarely	fall	
never	day	at { 6:00 / noon / night / midnight
	week	
	year	
	all the time	
	once a week	
	twice a month	
	3 times a year	
	once in a while	

Appendix 4B Present Progressive

now	this semester
right now	this evening
at the moment	this week
today	this year
these days	
nowadays	

Appendix 4C Past

YESTERDAY	LAST	AGO	IN/ON/AT
yesterday { morning, afternoon, evening }	last { night, week, month, year, summer }	{ an hour, two days, 6 months, a year } ago	in { 1988, June, the evening } on { Sunday, December 1, weekends } at { 6:00, night, midnight }

Appendix 4D Future

THIS	NEXT	TOMORROW	OTHER	IN/ON/AT
this { morning, afternoon, evening }	next { week, month, year, Sunday, weekend, summer }	tomorrow { morning, afternoon, evening, night }	soon later a week from today tonight for 3 days until 3:00	in { 15 minutes, a few days, 2 weeks, March, 2005 } on { Tuesday, May 21 } at { 4:00, midnight }

Appendix 5A   Subject Pronouns

SUBJECT PRONOUNS		
I	am	
He She It	is	happy.
We You They	are	

Appendix 5B   Object Pronouns

		OBJECT PRONOUNS
She	loves	me. him. her. it. us. you. them.

Appendix 5C   Demonstrative Pronouns

This That	is a grammar book.
These Those	are my classmates.

Appendix 5D   Possessive Pronouns

This book is	mine.
	his.
	hers.
	*
	ours.
	yours.
	theirs.

*It does not have a possessive pronoun.

Appendix 5E   Reflexive Pronouns

I		myself.
You		yourself.
We	love	ourselves.
You		yourselves.
They		themselves.
He		himself.
She	loves	herself.
It		itself.

Appendix 5F   Reciprocal Pronoun: *Each Other*

Friends	help	
They	are yelling at	each other.
Brad and Liz	love	
We	e-mailed	

Appendix 6A   Possessive Nouns

Bob's	
Thomas'	
Thomas's	
The teacher's	house is big.
The students'	
The children's	
Bob and Andrea's	

Appendix 6B   Possessive Determiners (Adjectives)

My	
His	
Her	
Its	eyes are big.
Our	
Your	
Their	

Appendix 6C   Possessive Pronouns

	mine.
	yours.
	his.
	hers.
The house is	*
	ours.
	yours.
	theirs.

*It does not have a possessive pronoun.

Appendix 7A Comparative Form (to compare two people, places, things, or actions)

| Betsy | is | older
bigger
busier
later
more punctual
less talkative | than | Judy. |
| | plays the violin | faster
more beautifully
better | | |

Appendix 7B Superlative Form (to compare one thing or person to all the others in a group)

| Betsy | is | the oldest
the biggest
the busiest
the most practical
the most punctual | of all her sisters. |
| | plays the violin | the fastest
more beautifully
the best | |

Appendix 7C *As . . . As* (to say that two people, places, or things are the same)

| Betsy | is | as | old
big
busy
practical
punctual | as | Judy. |
| | plays the violin | | fast
beautifully
well | | |

BASE FORM	SIMPLE PAST	PAST PARTICIPLE	BASE FORM	SIMPLE PAST	PAST PARTICIPLE
be	was	been	leave	left	left
become	became	become	lend	lent	lent
begin	began	begun	let	let	let
bend	bent	bent	lose	lost	lost
bite	bit	bitten	make	made	made
blow	blew	blown	meet	met	met
break	broke	broken	pay	paid	paid
bring	brought	brought	put	put	put
build	built	built	quit	quit	quit
buy	bought	bought	read	read*	read*
catch	caught	caught	ride	rode	ridden
choose	chose	chosen	ring	rang	rung
come	came	come	run	ran	run
cost	cost	cost	say	said	said
cut	cut	cut	see	saw	seen
dig	dug	dug	sell	sold	sold
do	did	done	send	sent	sent
draw	drew	drawn	shake	shook	shaken
drink	drank	drunk	shoot	shot	shot
drive	drove	driven	shut	shut	shut
eat	ate	eaten	sing	sang	sung
fall	fell	fallen	sit	sat	sat
feed	fed	fed	sleep	slept	slept
feel	felt	felt	speak	spoke	spoken
fight	fought	fought	spend	spent	spent
find	found	found	stand	stood	stood
fly	flew	flown	steal	stole	stolen
forget	forgot	forgotten	swim	swam	swum
get	got	gotten	take	took	taken
give	gave	given	teach	taught	taught
go	went	gone	tear	tore	torn
grow	grew	grown	tell	told	told
hang	hung	hung	think	thought	thought
have	had	had	throw	threw	thrown
hear	heard	heard	understand	understood	understood
hide	hid	hidden	wake	woke	woken
hit	hit	hit	wear	wore	worn
hold	held	held	win	won	won
hurt	hurt	hurt	write	wrote	written
keep	kept	kept			
know	knew	known			
lead	led	led			

*Pronounce the base form: /rid/; pronounce the past-tense form and the past participle: red.

UNIT 1

Unit 1, Opening Task (Page 1)

Go back to your guesses in the chart in the Task. Compare your guesses with the correct information below. Are your first impressions of each person correct?

NAME	AN PHAN	NAKISO MOYO	JACKIE VERAS	YOUNG MIN AND MI JUN KIM
Country	Vietnam	Zimbabwe	Dominican Republic	Korea
Nationality	Vietnamese	African	Dominican	Korean
Age	22	28	34	Young Min 50 Mi Jun 50
Single/Married/Divorced	single	single	divorced	married
Occupation	student	Web designer	secretary	shopkeepers

UNIT 3

Unit 3, Activity 1 (Page 42)

CATEGORIES					
	Monuments	Famous Places	Countries	Rivers, Mts, Deserts	Capitals
Question	*Where is/are...?*	*Where is/are...?*	*Where is...?*	*Where is/are...?*	*What's the capital of...?*
$10	People's Republic of China	Australia	Afghanistan	South America	Washington D.C.
$20	Greece	Zimbabwe and Zaire	Brazil	Mongolia and China	Santiago
$30	Moscow, Russia	The U.S.	Cuba	India	Rangoon
$40	Paris, France	Egypt	Greece	Nepal	Helsinki
$50	New York	Peru	India	Vietnam	Rabat

Unit 1, Activity 2 (Page 43)

Top row: Kofi Anan and Bono, The Dalai Lama, The Grand Canyon, Petronas Tower in Malaysia

Bottom row: Angkor Wat, Rio de Janeiro

APPENDIX 10   Exercises and Activities (Second Parts)

UNIT 1

Unit 1, Exercise 6 (Page 6)

List B

MEN	COUNTRY	NATIONALITY
1. Mario		Peruvian
2. Mohammed	Morocco	
3. Hideki and Yoshi		Japanese
4. Leonardo	the Dominican Republic	
5. Oumar		Senegalese

WOMEN	COUNTRY	NATIONALITY
6. Lilik	Indonesia	
7. Krystyna		Polish
8. Liisa and Katja	Finland	
9. Belen		Spanish
10. Margarita and Dalia	Brazil	
11. I		
12. You		

Unit 2, Exercise 4 (Page 18)

EXAMPLE:

1.

2.

3.

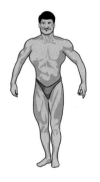

4.

5.

6.

7.

Unit 3, Exercise 7 (Page 34)

| Cloudy | Sunny | Partly cloudy | Rainy | Windy | Snowy |

MAP B

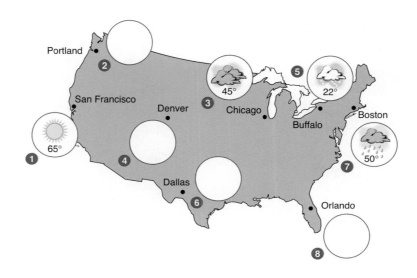

Unit 3, Exercise 8 (Page 36)

Chart B

STEP 1

1. 10:30   2. 6:15   3. 8:35   4. 11:45

STEP 2

5. 2:55   6. 4:10   7. 1:40   5. 3:20

PICTURE B

7.

sunglasses

8.

plane tickets

9.

address book

10.

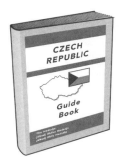

guide book

11.

suitcase

12.

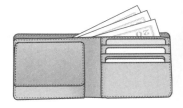

wallet

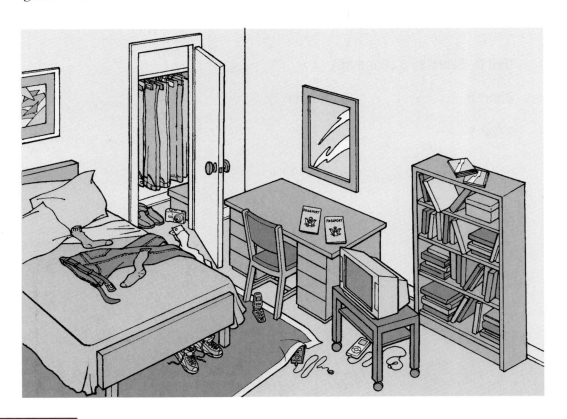

UNIT 9

Unit 9, Exercise 3 (Page 141)
Student B:

	ADRIANA		SANG-WOO	
	YES	NO	YES	NO
1. like to learn English			✔	
2. want to meet English-speaking people	✔			
3. feel nervous when speaking English			✔	
4. like to work in groups	✔			
5. need grammar rules to learn English			✔	
6. learn by speaking and listening to English	✔			
7. learn by reading and writing English			✔	
8. learn slowly, step by step		✔		
9. try new ways of learning				✔

UNIT 11

Unit 11, Exercise 10 (Page 181)

Yearly Consumption per Person in the United States in 2000
Chart B

CATEGORY	QUESTION
1. Meat (beef, pork, veal, lamb)	a. 195 pounds
2. Chicken	b.
3. Fish	c. 15 pounds
4. Milk	d.
5. Cheese	e.
6. Eggs	f. 250
7. Fats and Oils (vegetable oils, butter, margarine)	g. 74.5 pounds
8. Grain Products (bread, bakery items, etc.)	h.
9. Sugar	i. 152 pounds

Source: USDA

Unit 17, Exercise 9 (Page 281)

Chart B

1. Anne Frank		a. a young victim of the Nazis during World War II
		b. because she was Jewish
		c. her diary
2. Susan B. Anthony & Elizabeth Cady Stanton	d. who	
	e. what/famous for	
	f. when/famous	
3. Amelia Earhart		g. the first female aviator
		h. the first woman to fly across the Atlantic Ocean
		i. in 1928
4. Indira Gandhi	j. what/famous for	
	k. whose daughter	
	l. what/her father/famous for	

Unit 18, Exercise 15 (Page 307)

Text B

1. Doina grew up in _____ (where).
2. She married a government official.
3. She was pregnant in 1976. She had _____ (what).
4. Doina was unhappy _____ (why).
5. She thought of ways to escape every day.
6. She taught her daughter _____ (what).
7. On October 9, 1988, she and her daughter swam across the Danube River to Serbia.
8. _____ (who) caught them.
9. Doina and her daughter went to jail.
10. They tried to escape _____ (when) from jail.
11. Finally, they left Romania on foot in the middle of the night.
12. They flew to _____ (where) in 1989.
13. Doina went to school to learn English.
14. She wrote _____ (what) in her ESL class.

Unit 18, Exercise 12 (Page 303) and Activity 3 (Page 310)

The conclusion of Jerry's story:

Unit 18, Activity 6 (Page 311)

(Only the Host looks at this game board.)

Game Board

$$$	CATEGORY 1 PEOPLE	CATEGORY 2 *WH*-QUESTIONS	CATEGORY 3 *YES/NO* QUESTIONS
$10	Ms. Kudo	A flash drive	Yes, she did.
$20	Leo	On the first day of the new semester	Yes, he did.
$30	The Director	In her school bag	No, he didn't.
$40	Mr. Dim	Because he was jealous	No, he didn't.
$50	The students	She noticed grammar mistakes in the note.	Yes, they did.

Unit 24, Exercise 3 (Page 397)

Chart B

	NORTH AMERICA	SOUTH AMERICA	ASIA	EUROPE	AFRICA	THE WORLD
long river	The Mississippi		The Yangtze		The Nile	
large country		Brazil		Russia		Russia
populated country	The United States		The People's Republic of China		Nigeria	
high mountain		Mt. Aconcagua		Mt. Elbrus		Mt. Everest
small country	Bermuda		Macau		the Seychelles	

These are the words and phrases used in Unit 1 to greet, introduce, and say good-bye. Remember to add new phrases you hear to your Learning Journal.

Section 1: Words and Expressions

GREETINGS	RESPONSES	GOOD-BYES
Hello.		Have a good day.
Good morning.		Good-bye.
How do you do?	Very well, thank you.	So long.
How are you?		Take care.
How's everything?		See you later/tomorrow/next week.
How are you doing?	Fine, thank you.	Bye!
How's it going?	Great, thanks.	
What's happening?	Pretty good.	
Hi!	I'm okay.	
What's up?	I'm good.	
Hey!	So-so.	
What's new?	Not bad.	

PHOTO CREDITS

INDEX